不朽的美
似曾相识燕归来

许渊冲经典英译诗词

（五代——清朝）

第三辑：汉英对照

Songs of the Immortals

AN ANTHOLOGY OF CLASSICAL CHINESE POETRY (III)

Translated by Xu Yuan Zhong

许渊冲 译

新世界出版社
NEW WORLD PRESS

First Edition 2019

Translated by Xu Yuan Zhong
Designed by He Yuting

ISBN 978-7-5104-6281-8

Published by
NEW WORLD PRESS
24 Baiwanzhuang Street, Beijing 100037, China

Distributed by
NEW WORLD PRESS
24 Baiwanzhuang Street, Beijing 100037, China
Tel: 86-10-68995968
Fax: 86-10-68998705
Website: www.nwp.com.cn
E-mail: nwpcd@sina.com

Printed in the People's Republic of China

INTRODUCTION

"Chinese literature," according to John Turner in his *Golden Treasury of Chinese Poetry*, "is the high artistic peak of the most literary, the most artistic, the longest-established civilization that exists."

I

After the downfall of the Tang in 907, five short-lived dynasties were successively founded and overthrown from 907 to 960, and the unified empire was dismembered into ten independent sovereign states, of which the State of Shu in the west and that of the Southern Tang in the east were well-known for their literary achievements. When the regulated Tang verse could no longer adequately express man's more refined and delicate feelings, the tuned lyric of irregular line-length took its place and evolved into a major literary genre during the Five Dynasties. The literary aspect of the tuned lyric was derived from the five-character and seven-character lines of the regulated verse, the musical aspect from the popular songs and the tunes introduced from Central Asia, India and Myanmar. For example, *The*

Buddhist Dancers, one of the most popular tunes, was said to be a song in praise of the hairdress of the Myanmar empress of the time. So the tuned lyric may be considered as a result of intercultural communication.

As mentioned above, the states of Shu and Southern Tang were two cultural centers during the Five Dynasties period. In the former the first anthology of tuned lyrics appeared in 940, most of which can be called boudoir poetry in that it described beautiful heart-broken women in elegant chambers keeping cold, lonely beds beside a dimming candle or a solitary screen, in the waning spring or the dead of night, their lovers having gone far, far away.

Li Yu (937-978), the last ruler of the Southern Tang (937-975), represents the highest achievement of the lyric poets during the Five Dynasties period. His unusual accomplishment was closely related to his personal experiences. In his early years, as monarch, he indulged in a luxurious life at court. After losing his kingdom to the Song emperor in 976 and becoming a political prisoner in the Song capital, he lived a life of suffering until his death. His tragedy may be summed up in his tuned lyric written to the tune of *Dance of the Cavalry*, in which the expanse of his lost kingdom symbolizes the limitless extent of the universe and the short history of his dynasty becomes a universal symbol of the time past. The dominant theme in his lyric is no longer confined to the experiences of the inner chamber, but extends to embrace the historical dimension of a kingdom and the vast expanse of an empire. His individual experiences seem to gain universal importance. When compared with Wen and Wei, Li's poetry is more universal. Wen's lyrics are descriptive and static, Wei's narrative and active, while Li's more personal and emotional verses seem to view his own suffering in light of the destiny of all mankind. If Wen's lyrics are written with colored ink and Wei's with bitter tears, then Li's are composed of his heart's blood.

The tuned lyrics predominant in the Five Dynasties were short tunes divided into two stanzas and contained no more than 62 characters. The lyricists of the Northern Song (960-1127) included high officials and even prime ministers, who brought poetry into closer contact with the life of prosperous society in all its aspects-secular, intellectual and artistic. Premier Yan Shu (991-1055) and his son Yan Jidao (1030-1106) were both good at composing short tunes. Professor Chia-ying Yeh, who calls the son "poet of feeling" and the father "poet of intellect," says in *Song without Music*: "The one responds passively to life, registering experience as pure feeling; the other does not simply experience reality, and he contributes a ray of understanding to his experience. The response of the former suffers from its narrowness, where the latter has the advantage of breadth. Where the response is purely emotional, the poetry conveys emotion but lacks thought, making for superficiality, while the one who can illuminate his subject will include thought with his feelings, and the result is greater depth. Consider these lines by Yan Shu: "Deeply I sigh for faded flowers' fall in vain/Vaguely I seem to know the swallows come again." The observation of seasonal change is not just the occasion for an emotional response. The poet perceives a pattern, a contrast or a repetition, that gives a rational basis for the emotion.

Yan Shu may be regarded as the leader of early Northern Song poets, among whom figured Fan Zhongyan (989-1052), well-known for the quote that an ideal minister should be "first in worrying about the troubles of the world and last in enjoying its pleasures," and also known for his frontier lyrics. Ouyang Xiu (1007-1072), who sought spiritual sublimation in prose and emotional satisfaction in verse, was successful in enlarging the themes and the language of love poetry.

The short lyrics these poets wrote were as restricted in form as in content, for the restriction in form had its impact on content. It was Liu Yong (987-1053) who began to compose long lyrics or slow tunes, whose length ranges from 70 to 240 characters and which afford sufficient room for undulation and amplification. With the skilful use of this diversified form, he was able to transcend such conventional motifs as sorrows of love or remorse over separation and diverge from the domestic and the personal by giving voice to a deeper and more complex layer of meaning, to a wider horizon of the spiritual world, such as the sense of desolation and loftiness evoked by watching distant places in *Eight Beats of Ganzhou Song*. Thus in his hand the spirit and the outlook of the tuned lyric underwent a radical change, the rise of the long tunes becoming a major event in the evolution of the lyric.

The most important poet and lyricist of the Song Dynasty was Su Shi (Su Dongpo, 1037-1101). If the development of the tuned lyric in form may be attributed to Liu Yong, then its growth in content must be credited to Su Shi, who created the lyric in the mode of Tang poetry and in so doing broadened its scope and elevated its status to the extent that "there is no idea which cannot be expressed and there is no subject which cannot be treated" in his lyrics. His style is exuberant and spontaneous, characterized by his virile, unrestrained nature. His poetic diction ranges from colloquialism to classical expressions. His philosophy represents a combination of Confucianism and Taoism: "to serve the crown and to attain great renown" (*Spring in the Garden of Qin*) is his Confucian ideal and "to retire as times require" (*ibid*), and to be detached from gain and loss, his Taoist ideal. His philosophy can be seen in the following long lyric written to the tune of *Congratulations to the Bridegroom*:

Young swallows fly along the painted eaves
Which none perceives.
The shade of plane-trees keeps away
The hot noonday
And brings an evening fresh and cool
For the bathing lady beautiful.
She flirts a round fan of silk made,
Both fan and hand as white as jade.
Tired by and by,
She falls asleep with lonely sigh.
Who's knocking at the curtained door
That she can dream sweet dreams no more?
It is the gentle breeze who
Is again swaying green bamboo.
The pomegranate opens half her lips
Which look like wrinkled crimson strips;
When all the fickle flowers fade,
Alone she'll be the Beauty's maid.
How charming in her blooming branch, behold!

A fragrant heart seems wrapped a thousand fold.
But she's afraid to be surprised by western breeze
Which withers all the green leaves on the trees.
When you come to drink to the flower fair,
To see her withered too you cannot bear.
Then tears and flowers
Would fall in showers.

The bathing beauty is no longer the abandoned lady of palace poems, but an image of the purified soul of the disfavored poet still dreaming of his ideal unfulfilled, the pomegranate a symbol of the purified lady envied by all the fickle flowers. Here we see three images combined into one, that of a disappointed but not disillusioned intellectual.

Su Shi was considered to be the leader of the "heroic" school of lyrics, but he was also an innovator in writing lyrics of "delicate restraint," and Qin Guan (1049-1100), one of his followers, was regarded as representative of the "delicate" school. He was well-known for the following couplet:

If love between both sides can last for aye,
Why need they stay together night and day?

On the other hand, Zhou Bangyan (1057-1121), one of Liu Yong's followers, inherited the form from the master while at the same time surpassing his achievements. "While Su Shi remained an observer in creating a metaphorical relation between external objects and universal human feelings, Zhou developed a situation of poetic empathy in which the lyric self maintains a symbolic correspondence with external objects" (Kang-i Sun's *Evolution of Chinese Tz'u Poetry*). It is interesting to note that Zhou was once the rival of Emperor Hui Zong (Zhao Ji, 1082-1135) for the love of a singing girl Li Shishi (*Wandering of a Youth*). The emperor was himself a lyricist and wrote *Apricot Seen in the North* to the tune of *Hillside Pavilion* when he was a captive sent to the north by the Jurchen invaders. The descendant of the Song emperor who had captured Li Yu and put him to death was in turn captured and put to death by the Jurchen aggressors. Is it not true to say that justice has a long arm?

II

In 1125, when the Jurchen invaders marched south, the Song was forced to move its capital from Kaifeng to Hangzhou, south of the Yangtze River, which marked the beginning of the Southern Song Dynasty (1127-1279). Many patriots spoke out against the humiliation and called for military action to remedy it, thus Southern Song poetry possessed a patriotic fervor, of which General Yue Fei's (1103-1141) *The River All Red* is typical.

Li Qingzhao (1084-1151), who lived in the intervening period between the Northern and Southern Song, was the most remarkable lyric poetess of the Song Dynasty. Her lyrics recollect nostalgically her happy life in Kaifeng and reveal her distress in Hangzhou. "Her attempt to establish life in poetry was for her a stay against time, a surety to blot out oblivion. She tried to recapture the past, to preserve the present...." (*Sunflower Splendor*).

Lu You (1125-1210) was the best-known patriotic poet of the Southern Song. Even on his deathbed, he wrote the following quatrain exhorting his sons not to fail to report to his spirit at family sacrifices the news of the eventual recovery of the lost territory:

After my death I know for me all hopes are vain,
But still I'm grieved to see our country not unite.
When royal armies recover the Central Plain,
Do not forget to tell your sire in sacred rite!

Xin Qiji (1140-1207) was regarded as the most important lyric poet of the Southern Song Dynasty. He was a successor to Su Shi, continuing his thematic emphasis while at the same time putting a tighter rein on prosody than his master. It was not until his appearance that the tuned lyric flourished and reached its apex. His reputation as the best lyric poet of the "powerful and free" school rests on his heroic sentiments expressed in such lyrics as *The Partridge Sky and Dance of the Cavalry*.

On the other hand, among the lyric poets of the school of "delicate restraint," the best-known were Jiang Kui (1155-1221) and Wu Wenying (1200-1260). Successors to Zhou Bangyan, they had certain common features, such as their painstaking choice of words and phrases, and the great attention they paid to the music and the description of subtle feelings. But the content of their poems tended to be ambiguous, empty, and full of ornate classical allusions. As the tuned lyric became more and more concerned with technical details of embellishment, it gradually lost its vitality.

Towards the end of the Southern Song, the best-known poet of the "heroic" school was Wen Tianxiang (1236-1282), prime minister who led the royalist army to fight the Tartar invaders in 1275. Defeated and captured, he wrote the following verse on his way to Yanjing (present-day Beijing):

But I'll come back with blood oozing in cuckoo's cry.

He was executed in 1282 and with his death came the end of the Southern Song Dynasty.

III

During the one century of Mongol rule in the Yuan Dynasty (1271-1368), new musical melodies and new poetic genres emerged: song-poems, or non-dramatic songs, and dramatic songs. The new forms admit freely the use of everyday colloquial speech, the idiom and slang of the common people and extra words in addition to what was required by the melody. Writers of non-dramatic songs were skilled in their descriptions of sceneries and situations, persons and objects (though sometimes trivial and humorous) and thoughts and sentiments. But as a whole, the song-poem is basically lyrical in nature. On the other hand, dramatic songs are not only lyrical but also narrative. The most important writer of dramatic songs was Wang Shifu whose *Romance of the Western Chamber* contains a narrative part in prose and a lyrical part in verse. So the Yuan Dynasty may be considered one of transitional periods from predominance of poetry to that of prose. During the Ming Dynasty (1368-1644), narrative prose predominated over lyrical poetry, and it was not until the appearance of *A Dream of Red Mansions* in the Qing Dynasty (1644-1911) that the lyrical became as important as, if not more important than the narrative, but that question goes beyond the scope of the present book.

FIVE DYNASTIES

(907-960)

五代
（907—960）

NIU XI JI
(?-925)

Tune: "Mountain Hawthorn"*

Spring hills are casting off their misty veil.
The sky is lightening, the stars turn pale.
The parting moon vignettes a face in tears.
This dewy mom's the end of happy years.

Much has been said,
More's left unsaid.
She says again when round she turns her head,
"If you've this green silk skirt in mind,
To green grass you'll ne'er be unkind."

* Weng Xianliang's translation versified.

牛希济

（?–925）

生查子

春山烟欲收，天淡星稀小。
残月脸边明，别泪临清晓。

语已多，情未了，回首犹重道：
记得绿罗裙，处处怜芳草。

OUYANG JIONG
(895-971)

Tune: "Song of the Southern Country"

The sandy river shores extend far, far away.
The clouds are gilt by slanting sun on backward way.
By waterside the peacocks preen
Their tails gold-green;
Though startled, they won't stir when passers-by are seen.

欧阳炯

（*895–971*）

南乡子

岸远沙平，日斜归路晚霞明。
孔雀自怜金翠尾，临水，
认得行人惊不起。

GU XIONG
(Dates Unknown)

Tune: "Telling of Innermost Feeling"

Having deserted me,
Where hast thou gone from night to night?
No news of thee,
My scented chamber's closed tight.
My eyebrows knit,
The moon about to set,
How can I bear to think of it!
I loathe this lonely coverlet.
If thou exchanged thy heart for mine,
Then thou wouldst know how deep for thee I pine.

顾敻
（生卒年不详）

诉衷情

永夜抛人何处去？绝来音。
香阁掩，眉敛，月将沉。
争忍不相寻？怨孤衾。
换我心，为你心，始知相忆深。

LU QIANYI
(Dates Unknown)

Tune: "Immortal at the River"

All doors are double-locked; the garden waste is still.
Painted windows face the autumn sky, so sad and chill.
The royal flag has gone and left no trace; no flute is played
In bowers of jade,
Gone with the wind its broken tune.

The mist-veiled moon
Knows not the change of the world; it would peep
At dead of night into the palace deep.
In the wild pool red lotus blooms still stand;
They grieve in secret for the conquered land.
On fragrant petals dewdrops weep.

鹿虔扆
（生卒年不详）

临江仙

金锁重门荒苑静，绮窗愁对秋空。
翠华一去寂无踪。
玉楼歌吹，声断已随风。

烟月不知人事改，夜阑还照深宫。
藕花相向野塘中。
暗伤亡国，清露泣香红。

LI XUN
(855-930)

Tune: "Cloud Over Mount Witch"*

The ancient shrine still clings to the evergreen heights;
The wanton palace still lies there where waters wind.
The beauty's bower locked 'mid nature's delights,
Ghosts of romance and grandeur haunt my mind.

Each morning rosy clouds bring promise vain of bliss;
Each spring fresh buds awaken hopes of sweet fruition.
Why must these wailing monkeys come to me amiss?
A lonely trip's already a punition!

Tune: "Song of the Southern Country"

A skiff goes along
The lotus pond.
The sleeping lovebirds start at the oarswomen's song.
Perfumed girls lean upon each other making fun
And vie to be the fairest one.
They take round lotus leaves to shun
The setting sun.

* Weng Xianliang's translation versified. It was fabled that the king of Chu had a tryst with the Goddess of Mount Witch, who would come out in the morning in the form of a cloud and in the evening in the form of a shower over Mount Witch, the highest peak along the Yangtze River.

李珣
（*855–930*）

巫山一段云

古庙依青嶂，行宫枕碧流。
水声山色锁妆楼。往事思悠悠。

云雨朝还暮，烟花春复秋。
啼猿何必近孤舟？行客自多愁。

南乡子

乘彩舫，过莲塘，
棹歌惊起睡鸳鸯。
游女带花偎伴笑，争窈窕，
竞折团荷遮晚照。

FENG YANSI
(903-960)

Tune: "Butterflies Lingering Over Flowers"

Where have you gone like cloud from day to day,
Forgetting to come homeward way?
Don't you know spring's grown old and late?
Flowers and grass by roadside teem on Cold-Food Day.
Under whose tree's your scented cab and at whose gate?

Alone on balcony, with tearful eyes I query
A pair of returning swallows, dreary,
Whether they have met you on the pathway.
Spring sorrow's running wild like willow down, it seems;
Nowhere can I find you, e'en in my lonely dreams.

冯延巳
（903–960）

蝶恋花

几日行云何处去？
忘了归来，不道春将暮。
百草千花寒食路，香车系在谁家树？
泪眼倚楼频独语。
双燕飞来，陌上相逢否？
撩乱春愁如柳絮，依依梦里无寻处。

Tune: "Homage at the Golden Gate"

The breeze begins to blow,
Ruffling a pool of spring water below.
Crushing pink apricot petals in hand, I play
With a pair of lovebirds on the fragrant pathway.

Watching duck fight, alone on the railings I lean
Till slants upon my head my hairpin of jade green.
Waiting for you the whole day long wears out my eyes;
Raising my head, I'm glad to hear magpies.*

* Magpies were supposed to announce the expected arrival.

谒金门

风乍起，吹皱一池春水。
闲引鸳鸯香径里，手挼红杏蕊。

斗鸭阑干独倚，碧玉搔头斜坠。
终日望君君不至，举头闻鹊喜。

Tune: "Song of the Southern Country"

The raindrops glisten on the undulating grass,
With which my sorrow grows from year to year, alas!
In mist-veiled bower I have so much to regret
And never to forget.
The mirror and the quilt for a couple would make
My lonely heart break.

In dreams my soul may roam wherever it is led;
I wake to find the catkins o'er my broidered bed.
My fickle lover will no more
Enter my half-closed door.
The slanting sun would wring
Two streams of tears I owe him in departing spring.

南乡子

细雨湿流光，芳草年年与恨长。
烟锁凤楼无限事，茫茫。
鸾镜鸳衾两断肠。

魂梦任悠扬，睡起杨花满绣床。
薄悻不来门半掩，斜阳。
负你残春泪几行。

LI JING
(916-961) *

Tune: "Silk-Washing Stream"

The lotus flowers fade with blue-black leaves decayed;
The grievous western wind ripples the water green
As time will wrinkle faces fair. How can they bear,
Oh, to be seen!

In the fine rain she dreams of far-away frontiers;
Out of her bower wafts cold sound of flute of jade.
She leans with much regret and many, many tears
On balustrade.

* Second ruler of Southern Tang.

李璟
（916–961）

浣溪沙

菡萏香销翠叶残，西风愁起绿波间。
还与韶光共憔悴，不堪看。

细雨梦回鸡塞远，小楼吹彻玉笙寒。
多少泪珠何限恨，倚栏干。

LI YU
(937-978)*

Tune: "Pure, Serene Music"

Spring has half gone since we two parted,
I can see nothing now but brokenhearted.
Mume blossoms fall below the steps like whirling snow;
They cover me still though brushed off a while ago.

No message comes from the wild geese's song;**
In dreams you cannot come back, for the road is long.
The grief of separation is like spring grass,
Growing each day you're farther away, alas!

Tune: "Song of Picking Mulberries"

Red blooms are driven down by the departing spring,
Dancing while lingering.
My brows are knit again,
Though I try to unknit them in the drizzling rain.

No message comes to lonely windows all the day,
The incense burned to ashes grey.
How can I from spring thoughts be free?
I try to sleep, but in my dream spring comes to me.

* Son of Li Jing and last ruler of Southern Tang.
** The wild geese were supposed to be messengers in ancient China.

李煜

（937–978）

清平乐

别来春半，触目柔肠断。
砌下落梅如雪乱，拂了一身还满。

雁来音信无凭，路遥归梦难成。
离恨恰如春草，更行更远还生。

采桑子

亭前春逐红英尽，舞态徘徊。
细雨霏微，不放双眉时暂开。

绿窗冷静芳音断，香印成灰。
可奈情怀，欲睡朦胧入梦来。

Tune: "Migrant Orioles"

The morning moon is sinking;
Few clouds are floating there;
I lean upon my pillow with no word.
E'en in my dream I'm thinking
Of the green grass so fair,
But from afar the wild geese are not heard.

Orioles no longer sing their song;
Late vernal blooms are whirling around.
In courtyard as in painted hall
Solitude reigns the whole night long.
Don't sweep away the fallen blossoms on the ground!
Leave them there till the dancer comes back from the ball!

喜迁莺

晓月坠，宿云微，无语枕频欹。
梦回芳草思依依，天远雁声稀。

啼莺散，余花乱，寂寞画堂深院。
片红休扫尽从伊，留待舞人归。

Tune: "Buddhist Dancers"

Bright flowers bathed in thin mist and dim moonlight,
'Tis best time to steal out to see my love tonight.*
With stocking feet on fragrant steps I tread,
Holding in hand my shoes sown with gold thread.

We meet south of the painted hall,
And trembling in his arms I fall.
"It's hard for me to come o'er here,
So you may love your fill, my dear!"

Tune: "Dance of the Cavalry"

A reign of forty years
O'er land and hills and streams,
My royal palace touching the celestial spheres,
My shady forest looking deep like leafy dreams.
What did I know of shields and spears?

A captive now, I'm worn away;
Thinner I grow; my hair turns grey.
Oh, how can I forget the hurried parting day
When by the band the farewell songs were played
And I shed tears before my palace maid!

* A tryst between the poet-king and the younger sister of the queen.

菩萨蛮

花明月暗笼轻雾，今宵好向郎边去。
刬袜步香阶，手提金缕鞋。

画堂南畔见，一向偎人颤。
奴为出来难，教君恣意怜。

破阵子

四十年来家国，三千里地山河。
凤阁龙楼连霄汉，玉树琼枝作烟萝。
几曾识干戈？

一旦归为臣虏，沈腰潘鬓消磨。
最是仓皇辞庙日，教坊犹奏别离歌，
垂泪对宫娥。

Tune: “Midnight Song”

From sorrow and regret our life cannot be free.
Why is this soul-consuming grief e’er-haunting me!
I went to my lost land in dreams;
Awake, I find tears flow in streams.

Who would ascend again those towers high?
I can’t forget those autumn days gone by.
Vain is the happiness of yore;
It melts like dreams and is no more.

Tune: “The Beautiful Lady Yu”

When will there be no more autumn moon and spring flowers
For me who had so many memorable hours?
My attic, which last night in vernal wind did stand,
Reminds me cruelly of the lost moonlit land.

Carved balustrades and marble steps must still be there,
But rosy faces cannot be as fair.
If you ask me how much my sorrow has increased,
Just see the over-brimming river flowing east!

子夜歌

人生愁恨何能免，销魂独我情何限！
故国梦重归，觉来双泪垂。

高楼谁与上？长记秋晴望。
往事已成空，还如一梦中。

虞美人

春花秋月何时了？往事知多少。
小楼昨夜又东风，故国不堪回首月明中。

雕栏玉砌应犹在，只是朱颜改。
问君能有几多愁？恰似一江春水向东流。

Tune: "Ripples Sifting Sand"

The curtain cannot keep out the patter of rain;
Springtime is on the wane.
In the deep of night my quilt is not cold-proof.
Forgetting I am under hospitable roof,
Still in my dream I seek for pleasure vain.

Don't lean alone on railings and
Yearn for the boundless land!
To bid farewell is easier than to meet again.
With flowers fallen on the waves spring's gone away;
So has the paradise of yesterday!

Tune: "Joy of Meeting"

Spring's rosy color fades from forest flowers
Too soon, too soon.
How can they bear cold morning showers
And winds at noon?

Her rouged tears like crimson rain
Intoxicate my heart.
When shall we meet again?
As water eastward flows, so shall we part.

浪淘沙

帘外雨潺潺，春意阑珊。罗衾不耐五更寒。
梦里不知身是客，一晌贪欢。

独自莫凭栏，无限江山，
别时容易见时难。
流水落花春去也，天上人间。

相见欢

林花谢了春红，太匆匆。
无奈朝来寒雨晚来风。

胭脂泪，留人醉，几时重。
自是人生长恨水长东。

Tune: "Ripples Sifting Sand"

It saddens me to think of days gone by,
With old familiar scenes in my mind's eye.
The autumn wind is blowing hard
O'er moss-grown steps in deep courtyard.
Let beaded screen hang idly unrolled at the door.
Who will come any more?

Sunk and buried my golden armor lies;
Amid o'ergrowing weeds my vigor dies.
The blooming moon is rising in the evening sky.
The palaces of jade
With marble balustrade
Are reflected in vain on the River Qinhuai.

浪淘沙

往事只堪哀，对景难排。秋风庭院藓侵阶。
一任珠帘闲不卷，终日谁来？

金锁已沉埋，壮气蒿莱。
晚凉天净月华开。
想得玉楼瑶殿影，空照秦淮。

Tune: "Joy of Meeting"

Silent, I climb the western tower alone,
But see the hooklike moon.
The plane-trees lonesome and drear
Lock in the courtyard autumn clear.

Cut, it won't sever;
Be ruled, 'twill never.
What sorrow 'tis to part!
It's an unspeakable taste in the heart.

Tune: "Crows Cawing at Night"

Wind soughed and rain fell all night long;
Door curtains rustled like an autumn song.
The water clock drip-dropping and the candle dying,
I lean on pillow troubled, sitting up or lying.

All are gone with the running stream;
My floating life is but a dream.
Let wine cups be my surest haunt;
On nothing else can I e'er count.

相见欢

无言独上西楼，月如钩。
寂寞梧桐深院锁清秋。

剪不断，理还乱，是离愁。
别是一般滋味在心头。

乌夜啼

昨夜风兼雨，帘帏飒飒秋声。
烛残漏断频欹枕，起坐不能平。

世事漫随流水，算来一梦浮生。
醉乡路稳宜频到，此外不堪行。

SONG DYNASTY

(960-1279)

宋朝

(960—1279)

LADY PISTIL
(Dates Unknown)

Written at the Capitulation of the Kingdom of Shu*

My lord erected "surrender flag" on city wall.
How could a woman living deep in palace know?
They were disarmed, one hundred forty thousand men in all;
Not one of them was man enough to fight the foe.

* The ruler of Shu surrendered to the first emperor of the Song Dynasty in 965. His favorite Lady Pistil was famed for her poetry; the emperor ordered her to write the above poem impromptu.

花蕊夫人
（生卒年不详）

述国亡诗

君王城上竖降旗，
妾在深宫那得知？
十四万人齐解甲，
更无一个是男儿！

ZHENG WENBAO
(952-1012)

Tune: "Willow-Branch Song"

The painted ship on vernal lake has tarried long;
Until half-drunk no one will sing a farewell song.
At last the sorrow-laden ship goes on before
Through mist and rain, through wind and wave to southern shore.

郑文宝

（*952–1012*）

柳枝词

亭亭画舸系春潭，
直到行人酒半酣。
不管烟波与风雨，
载将离恨过江南。

LIN BU
(967-1028)

To the Mume Blossom

You bloom alone when flowers fade out far and near;
You queen it over all the garden day and night.
Sparse shadows slant across the shallow water clear;
Your gloomy fragrance floats at dusk in dim moonlight.
Seeing your purity, white birds alight and peer;
Knowing your sweetness, butterflies lose their heart.
Only a lucky poet's your companion dear.
Put sandal clappers and golden goblets apart!*

* Singers and drinkers are not your good companions.

林逋

（967–1028）

梅花

众芳摇落独暄妍，占尽风情向小园。
疏影横斜水清浅，暗香浮动月黄昏。
霜禽欲下先偷眼，粉蝶如知合断魂。
幸有微吟可相狎，不须檀板共金尊。

PAN LANG
(?-1009)

Tune: "Fountain of Wine"

I still remember watching tidal bore;
The city poured out people on the shore.
It seemed the sea had emptied all its water here,
And thousands of drums were beating far and near.

At the crest of huge billows the swimmers did stand,
Yet dry remained red flags they held in hand.
Back, I saw in dreams the tide o'erflow the river;
Awake, I feel my heart with cold still shiver.

潘阆
（?–1009）

酒泉子

长忆观潮，满郭人争江上望。
来疑沧海尽成空，万面鼓声中。

弄潮儿向涛头立，手把红旗旗不湿。
别来几向梦中看，梦觉尚心寒。

LIU YONG
(987-1053)

Tune: "Joy of Day and Night"

In nuptial chamber first I saw your face;
I thought we should forever share the place.
The short-lived joy of love, who would believe?
Soon turned to parting that would grieve.
Now late spring has grown old and soon takes leave;
I see a riot of catkins and flowers
Fallen in showers.
I am afraid all the fine scenery
Will go away with thee.

Whom may I tell my solitude?
Thou oft makest light of promise thou hast made.
Had I known the ennui is so hard to elude,
I would then have thee stayed.
What I can't bear to think, thy gallantry apart,
Is something else in thee that captivates my heart.
If one day I don't think of it,
A thousand times my brows will knit.

柳永

（987–1053）

昼夜乐

洞房记得初相遇，便只合长相聚。
何期小会幽欢，变作离情别绪。
况值阑珊春色暮，对满目乱花狂絮。
直恐好风光，尽随伊归去。

一场寂寞凭谁诉？算前言总轻负。
早知恁地难拚，悔不当时留住。
其奈风流端正外，更别有，系人心处。
一日不思量，也攒眉千度。

Tune: "Bells Ringing in the Rain"

Cicadas chill
Drearily shrill.
We stand face to face at an evening hour
Before the pavilion, after a sudden shower.
Can we care for drinking before we part?
At the city gate
We are lingering late,
But the boat is waiting for you to depart.
Hand in hand, we gaze at each other's tearful eyes
And burst into sobs with words congealed on our lips.
You'll go your way
Far, far away
On miles and miles of misty waves where sail the ships
And evening clouds hang low in boundless southern skies.

Lovers would grieve at parting as of old.
How could you stand this clear autumn day so cold!
Where will you be found at daybreak
From wine awake?
Moored by a riverbank planted with willow trees
Beneath the waning moon and in the morning breeze.
You'll be gone for a year.
What could I do with all bright days and fine scenes here!
Howe'er coquettish I am on my part,
To whom can I lay bare my heart?

雨霖铃

寒蝉凄切，对长亭晚，骤雨初歇。
都门帐饮无绪，留恋处，兰舟催发。
执手相看泪眼，竟无语凝噎。
念去去，千里烟波，暮霭沉沉楚天阔。

多情自古伤离别，更那堪，冷落清秋节！
今宵酒醒何处？杨柳岸，晓风残月。
此去经年，应是良辰好景虚设。
便纵有千种风情，更与何人说？

Tune: "Eight Beats of Ganzhou Song"

Shower by shower
The evening rain besprinkles the sky
Over the river,
Washing cool the autumn air both far and nigh.
Gradually frost falls and blows the wind so chill
That few people pass by the hill or rill.
In fading sunlight drowned is my bower.
Everywhere the red and the green wither away,
There's no more splendor of a sunny day.
Only the waves of River Long
Silently eastward flow along.

I cannot bear
To climb high and look far, for to gaze where
My native land is lost in mists so thick
Would make my lonely heart homesick.
I sigh over the paths I've traversed year by year.
Why should I linger hopelessly now there, now here?
From her bower my lady fair
Must gaze with longing eye.
How oft has she mistaken homebound sails
On the horizon for mine?
How could she know that I,
Leaning upon the rails,
With sorrow frozen on my face, for her do pine!

八声甘州

对潇潇暮雨洒江天，一番洗清秋。
渐霜风凄紧，关河冷落，残照当楼。
是处红衰翠减，苒苒物华休。
唯有长江水，无语东流。

不忍登高临远，望故乡渺邈，归思难收。
叹年来踪迹，何事苦淹留？
想佳人，妆楼颙望，误几回天际识归舟。
争知我，倚栏杆处，正恁凝愁！

Tune: "Imperial Capital Recalled"

In thin quilt on small pillow when weather is cold,
I begin to feel now the parting sorrow deep.
I toss from side to side until night has grown old;
I get up and lie down, but I can't fall asleep.
The night seems to appear
As long as a whole year.

I want to go back to see you and stay,
But I'm already far away.
Thousands of thoughts and lame excuses only
Make me feel all the more weary and lonely.
I shall miss you for the rest of my years,
Which can't compensate you for all your tears.

忆帝京

薄衾小枕凉天气，乍觉别离滋味。
辗转数寒更，起了还重睡。
毕竟不成眠，一夜长如岁。

也拟待、却回征辔，又争奈、已成行计。
万种思量，多方开解，只恁寂寞厌厌地。
系我一生心，负你千行泪。

FAN ZHONGYAN
(989-1052)

Tune: "Screened by Southern Curtain"

Emerald clouds above
And yellow leaves below,
O'er autumn-tinted waves, cold, green mists grow.
The sun slants o'er the hills; the sky and waves seem one;
Unfeeling grass grows sweet beyond the setting sun.

A homesick heart
Lost in thoughts deep,
Only sweet dreams each night can retain me in sleep.
Don't lean alone on rails when the bright moon appears!
Wine in sad bowels would turn into nostalgic tears.

范仲淹

（989–1052）

苏幕遮

碧云天，黄叶地。
秋色连波，波上寒烟翠，
山映斜阳天接水。
芳草无情，更在斜阳外。

黯乡魂，追旅思，
夜夜除非，好梦留人睡。
明月楼高休独倚，
酒入愁肠，化作相思泪。

ZHANG XIAN
(990-1078)

Tune: "Song of the Immortal"

Wine cup in hand, I listen to "The Water Song,"
Awake from wine at noon but not from sorrow long.
When will spring come back now it is going away?
In the mirror, alas!
I see happy time pass.
In vain may I recall the old days gone for aye.

Night falls on poolside sand where pairs of lovebirds stay;
The moon breaks through the clouds; with shadows flowers play.
Lamplight is veiled by screen on screen;
The fickle wind still blows,
The night quite silent grows.
Tomorrow fallen blooms on the way will be seen.

张先
（990–1078）

天仙子

水调数声持酒听，午醉醒来愁未醒。
送春春去几时回？临晚镜，伤流景，
往事后期空记省。

沙上并禽池上暝，云破月来花弄影。
重重帘幕密遮灯。风不定，人初静，
明日落红应满径。

YAN SHU
(991-1055)

Tune: "Silk-Washing Stream"*

I compose a new song and drink a cup of wine
In the bower of last year when weather is as fine.
When will you come back like the sun on the decline?

Deeply I sigh for faded flowers' fall in vain;
Vaguely I seem to know the swallows come again.
Loitering on the garden path, I alone remain.

* Written for a singing girl.

晏殊
（991–1055）

浣溪沙

一曲新词酒一杯，去年天气旧亭台。
夕阳西下几时回？

无可奈何花落去，似曾相识燕归来。
小园香径独徘徊。

ZHANG BIAN
(992-1077)

Tune: "Swallows Leaving Pavilion"

So picturesque the land by riverside,
In autumn tints the scenery is purified.
Without a break green waves merge into azure sky;
The sunbeams after rain take chilly dye.
Bamboo fence dimly seen on islets 'mid the reeds
And thatched cottages on the shore o'ergrown with weeds.

Among white clouds are lost white sails,
And where smoke coils up slow,
There wine shop flag hangs low.
How many of the fisherman's and woodman's tales
Are told about the Six Dynasties' fall and rise!*
Saddened, I lean upon the tower's rails;
Mutely the sun turns cold and sinks in western skies.

* Written at Jinling, capital of the Six Dynasties (221-280; 317-589).

张昇

（992–1077）

离亭燕

一带江山如画，风物向秋潇洒。
水浸碧天何处断？霁色冷光相射。
蓼屿荻花洲，掩映竹篱茅舍。

云际客帆高挂，烟外酒旗低亚。
多少六朝兴废事，尽入渔樵闲话。
怅望倚层楼，寒日无言西下。

SONG QI
(998-1061)

Tune: "Lily Magnolia Flowers"

The scenery is getting fine east of the town;
The rippling water greets boats rowing up and down.
Beyond green willows morning chill is growing mild;
On pink apricot branches spring is running wild.
In our floating life scarce are pleasures we seek after.
How can we value gold above hearty laughter?
I raise wine cup to ask the slanting sun to stay
And leave among the flowers its departing ray.

宋祁

（*998–1061*）

木兰花

东城渐觉风光好，縠皱波纹迎客棹。
绿杨烟外晓寒轻，红杏枝头春意闹。
浮生长恨欢娱少，肯爱千金轻一笑？
为君持酒劝斜阳，且向花间留晚照。

OUYANG XIU
(1007-1072)

Tune: "Treading on Grass"

Roadside mume blossoms fade,
Riverside willows green,
On fragrant grass in the warm air a rider's seen.
The farther he goes, the longer his parting grief grows;
Endless like water in vernal river it flows.

With broken, tender heart
And tearful, longing eye,
His wife won't lean on railings of the tower high.
Beyond the far-flung plain mountains shut out her view;
The rider's farther away than the mountains blue.

欧阳修

（1007–1072）

踏莎行

候馆梅残，溪桥柳细，草薰风暖摇征辔。
离愁渐远渐无穷，迢迢不断如春水。

寸寸柔肠，盈盈粉泪，楼高莫近危栏倚。
平芜尽处是春山，行人更在春山外。

Tune: "Butterflies Lingering Over Flowers"

Deep, deep the courtyard where he is, so deep
It's veiled by smoky willows heap on heap,
By curtain on curtain and screen on screen.
Leaving his saddle and bridle, there he has been
Merrymaking. From my tower his trace can't be seen.

The third moon now, the wind and rain are raging late;
At dusk I bar the gate,
But I can't bar in spring.
My tearful eyes ask flowers, but they fail to bring
An answer; I see red blossoms fly o'er the swing.

蝶恋花

庭院深深深几许？
杨柳堆烟，帘幕无重数。
玉勒雕鞍游冶处，楼高不见章台路。

雨横风狂三月暮。
门掩黄昏，无计留春住。
泪眼问花花不语，乱红飞过秋千去。

ZENG GONG
(1019-1083)

The West Tower

The billows come and go like cloud;
The north wind blows up thunder loud.
All curtains rolled up in west tower;
From hill on hill comes sudden shower.

曾巩
（*1019–1083*）

西楼

海浪如云去却回，
北风吹起数声雷。
朱楼四面钩疏箔，
卧看千山急雨来。

SIMA GUANG
(1019-1086)

Tune: "The Moon over the West River"

Loosely she has done up her hair;
Thinly she has powdered her face.
In rosy smoke and purple mist she looks so fair;
As light as willow down she walks with grace.
Before we part, we long to meet;
Amorous, she seems not in love.
Awake from wine and songs so sweet,
She finds the courtyard still and bright the moon above.

司马光
（1019–1086）

西江月

宝髻松松挽就，铅华淡淡妆成。
青烟翠雾罩轻盈，飞絮游丝无定。
相见争如不见，多情还似无情。
笙歌散后酒微醒，深院月明人静。

WANG ANSHI
(1021-1086)

Tune: "Fragrance of Laurel Branch"

I climb a height
And strain my sight;
Of autumn late it is the coldest time;
The ancient capital looks sublime.
The limpid river, belt-like, flows a thousand miles;
Emerald peak on peak towers in piles.
In the declining sun sails come and go;
In the west wind wine shop flags flutter high and low.
The painted boat
In clouds afloat,
Like stars in Silver River* egrets fly.
What a picture before the eye!

The days gone by
Saw people in opulence vie.
Alas! Shame came on shame under the walls,**
In palace halls.
Leaning on rails, in vain I utter sighs
O'er ancient kingdoms' fall and rise.
The running water saw the Six Dynasties pass,
But I see only chilly mist and withered grass.
E'en now the songstresses still sing
The songs composed by captive king.

---

* The Chinese name for the Milky Way.
** Rulers capitulated under the walls of their capital during the Six Dynasties (221-280; 317-589).

王安石

（1021–1086）

桂枝香

登临送目，正故国晚秋，天气初肃。
千里澄江似练，翠峰如簇。
归帆去棹残阳里，背西风，酒旗斜矗。
彩舟云淡，星河鹭起，画图难足。

念往昔，繁华竞逐，叹门外楼头，悲恨相续。
千古凭高对此，谩嗟荣辱。
六朝旧事随流水，但寒烟衰草凝绿。
至今商女，时时犹唱，后庭遗曲。

Tune: "Song of the Southern Country"

The capital was ruled by kings since days gone by.
The rich green and lush gloom breathe a majestic sigh.
Like dreams has passed the reign of four hundred long years,
Which calls forth tears.
Modern laureates are buried like their ancient peers.

Along the river I go where I will,
Up city walls and watch towers I gaze my fill.
Do not ask what has passed without leaving a trail!
To what avail?
The endless river rolls in vain beyond the rail.

南乡子

自古帝王州，郁郁葱葱佳气浮。
四百年来成一梦，堪愁！
晋代衣冠成古丘。

绕水恣行游。上尽层城更上楼。
往事悠悠君莫问，回头！
槛外长江空自流。

WANG ANGUO
(1028-1074)

Tune: "Shortened Form of Lily Magnolia Flowers"

'Neath painted bridge water flows by;
The fallen flowers wet with rain can no more fly.
The moon breaks through twilight;
Fragrance within the curtain's smelt ere I alight.

Silently lingering around,
Where will my dreaming soul tonight be found?
Unlike the weeping willow,
Whose down will fly into your room and on your pillow.

王安国

（1028–1074）

减字木兰花

画桥流水。雨湿落红飞不起。
月破黄昏。帘里余香马上闻。

徘徊不语，今夜梦魂何处去？
不似垂杨，犹解飞花入洞房。

YAN JIDAO
(1030-1106)

Tune: "Immortal at the River"

Awake from dreams, I find the locked tower high;
Sobered from wine, I see the curtain hanging low.
As last year spring grief seems to grow;
Amid the falling blooms alone stand I;
In the fine rain a pair of swallows fly.

I still remember when I first saw pretty Ping*
In silken dress embroidered with two hearts in a ring,
Revealing lovesickness by touching pipa's string.
The moon shines bright just as last year;
It did see her like a cloud disappear.

* A pipa player.

晏几道
（*1030–1106*）

临江仙

梦后楼台高锁，酒醒帘幕低垂。
去年春恨却来时。
落花人独立，微雨燕双飞。

记得小蘋初见，两重心字罗衣。
琵琶弦上说相思。
当时明月在，曾照彩云归。

Tune: "Partridge Sky"

Time and again with colored sleeves you tried to fill
My cup with wine that, drunk, I kept on drinking still.
You danced until the moon hung low o'er willow trees;
You sang until amid peach blossoms blushed the breeze.

Then came the time to part,
But you're deep in my heart.
How many times have I met you in dreams at night!
Now left to gaze at you in silver candlelight,
I fear it is not you
But a sweet dream untrue.

鹧鸪天

彩袖殷勤捧玉钟，当年拚却醉颜红。
舞低杨柳楼心月，歌尽桃花扇底风。

从别后，忆相逢，几回魂梦与君同。
今宵剩把银釭照，犹恐相逢是梦中。

CHENG HAO (1032-1085)

Impromptu Lines on a Spring Day

Towards noon 'neath fleecy clouds and gentle breeze
I cross the stream 'mid blooms and willow trees.
Some worldlings who don't know my heart's deep pleasure
Would say I'm like a truant fond of leisure.

程颢

（1032–1085）

春日偶成

云淡风轻近午天，
傍花随柳过前川。
时人不识余心乐，
将谓偷闲学少年。

WANG GUAN
(Dates Unknown)

Tune: "Song of Divination"

A stretch of rippling water is a beaming eye;
The arched brows around are mountains high.
If you ask where the wayfarer is bound,
Just see where beaming eyes and arched brows are found.

I've just seen spring depart,
And now with you I'll part.
If you o'ertake in the south the spring flay,
Oh! Be sure not to let it slip away!

王观
（生卒年不详）

卜算子

水是眼波横，山是眉峰聚。
欲问行人去那边？眉眼盈盈处。

才始送春归，又送君归去。
若到江南赶上春，千万和春住。

SU SHI
(1037-1101)

Drinking at the Lake, First in Sunny, Then Rainy Weather

The brimming waves delight the eye on sunny days;
The dimming hills present rare view in rainy haze.
West Lake may be compared to Beauty of the West;*
It becomes her to be adorned or plainly drest.

* Xi Shi, a beautiful lady of the 5th century BC born near West Lake.

苏轼

（1037–1101）

饮湖上初晴后雨

水光潋滟晴方好，
山色空濛雨亦奇。
欲把西湖比西子，
淡妆浓抹总相宜。

Tune: "Spring in the Garden of Qin"

*Written to My Brother on My Way to Mizhou**

The lamp burns with green flames in an inn's lonely hall;
Wayfarers' dreams are broken by the cock's loud call.
Slowly the blooming moon rolls up her silk dress white;
The frost begins to shimmer in the soft daylight;
The cloud-crowned hills outspread their rich brocade
And morning dewdrops gleam like pearls displayed.
As the way of the world is long,
But toilsome life is short,
So, for a man like me, joyless is oft my sort.
After humming this song,
Silent, on my saddle I lean,
Brooding over the past, scene after scene.

Together to the capital we came,
Like the two brothers Lu of literary fame.
A fluent pen combined
With a widely read mind,
Why could we not have helped the crown
To attain great renown?
As times require,
We advance or retire;
With folded arms we may stand by.
If we keep fit,
We may enjoy life before we lose it.
So drink the wine cup dry!

* Mizhou was a poor district where officials under a cloud were sent.

沁园春

赴密州，早行，马上寄子由

孤馆灯青，野店鸡号，旅枕梦残。
渐月华收练。晨霜耿耿，云山摛锦，朝露漙漙。
世路无穷，劳生有限，似此区区长鲜欢。
微吟罢，凭征鞍无语，往事千端。

当时共客长安，似二陆初来俱少年。
有笔头千字，胸中万卷，致君尧舜，此事何难。
用舍由时，行藏在我，袖手何妨闲处看。
身长健，但优游卒岁，且斗樽前。

Tune: "A Riverside Town"

*Dreaming of my deceased wife on the night of the twentieth day of the first moon**

For ten long years the living of the dead knows naught.
Though to my mind not brought,
Could the dead be forgot?
Her lonely grave is far, a thousand miles away.
To whom can I my grief convey?
Revived, e'en if she be, oh, could she still know me?
My face is worn with care
And frosted is my hair.

Last night I dreamed of coming to our native place;
She's making up her face
Before her mirror with grace.
Each saw the other hushed,
But from our eyes tears gushed.
When I am woken, oh, I know I'll be heartbroken
Each night when the moon shines
O'er her grave clad with pines.

---

* In 1075 the poet dreamed of his first wife, Wang Fu, whom he married in 1054 and who died in 1065.

江城子·乙卯正月二十日夜记梦

十年生死两茫茫，不思量，自难忘。
千里孤坟，无处话凄凉。
纵使相逢应不识，尘满面，鬓如霜。

夜来幽梦忽还乡，小轩窗，正梳妆。
相顾无言，惟有泪千行。
料得年年肠断处，明月夜，短松冈。

Tune: "Prelude to Water Melody"

On the night of the Mid-autumn Festival of 1076 I drank happily till dawn and wrote this in my cups while thinking of my brother.

How long will the full moon appear?
Wine cup in hand, I ask the sky.
I do not know what time of year
'Twould be tonight in the palace on high.
Riding the wind, there I would fly,
Yet I'm afraid the crystalline palace would be
Too high and cold for me.
I rise and dance; with my shadow I play.
On high as on earth, would it be as gay?

The moon goes round the mansions red
Through gauze-draped windows soft to shed
Her light upon the sleepless bed.
Against man she should have no spite.
Why, then, when people part, is she oft full and bright?
Men have sorrow and joy; they part or meet again;
The moon is bright or dim and she may wax or wane.
There has been nothing perfect since the olden days.
So let us wish that man
Will live long as he can!
Though miles apart, we'll share the beauty she displays.

水调歌头

丙辰中秋，欢饮达旦，大醉，作此篇，兼怀子由。

明月几时有？把酒问青天。
不知天上宫阙，今夕是何年？
我欲乘风归去，又恐琼楼玉宇，高处不胜寒。
起舞弄清影，何似在人间？

转朱阁，低绮户，照无眠。
不应有恨，何事长向别时圆？
人有悲欢离合，月有阴晴圆缺，此事古难全。
但愿人长久，千里共婵娟。

The Hundred-Pace Rapids

*When Wang Ding-guo was visiting me at Pengcheng (Xuzhou), he went one day with Yan Fu in a small boat, accompanied by three singing girls, for an outing on the River Si. To the north they climbed Holy Woman Hill; southward they poled down the Hundred-Pace Rapids, playing flutes, drinking wine, and returning home by moonlight. I had business to attend to and could not go with them, but when evening came and I had changed into informal Taoist robes, I stood at the top of the Yellow Tower and gazed in the direction they had gone, laughing and thinking to myself that not since the poet Li Bai had died some three hundred years ago had there been such a merry expedition. Wang Ding-guo went away, and the following month Abbot Can-liao and I poled down those same rapids, thinking of that earlier outing, which now seemed like an event of the distant past. Sighing to myself, I composed these two poems. One I gave to Abbot Can-liao, the other I sent to Wang Ding-guo.**

Waves leap up where the long, long rapids steeply fall;
A light boat southward shoots like plunging shuttle, lo!
Water birds fly up at the boatman's desperate call.
Among the rocks it strives to thread its way and go
As a hare darts away, an eagle dives below,
A gallant steed runs down a slope beyond control,
A string snaps from a lute, an arrow from a bow,
Lightning cleaves clouds or off lotus leaves raindrops roll.
The mountains whirl around, the wind sweeps by the ear,
I see the current boil in a thousand whirlpools.
At the risk of my life I feel a joy without peer,
Just like the god who boasts of the river he rules.

*Not selected in this anthology.

百步洪

王定国访余于彭城，一日，棹小舟与颜长道携盼、英、卿三子，游泗水，北上圣女山，南下百步洪，吹笛饮酒，乘月而归。余时以事不得往，夜著羽衣，伫立于黄楼上，相视而笑。以为李太白死，世间无此乐三百余年矣。定国既去逾月，复与参寥师放舟洪下，追怀曩游，以为陈迹，肖然而叹。故作二诗，一以遗参寥，一以寄定国，且示颜长道、舒尧文邀同赋云。

长洪斗落生跳波，轻舟南下如投梭。
水师绝叫凫雁起，乱石一线争磋磨。
有如兔走鹰隼落，骏马下注千丈坡。
断弦离柱箭脱手，飞电过隙珠翻荷。
四山眩转风掠耳，但见流沫生千涡。
险中得乐虽一快，何异水伯夸秋河。

Our life will pass like water running day and night;
Our thoughts can in a twinkling go beyond ninth sphere.
Many people in drunken dreams contend and fight.
Do they know palaces 'mid weeds will disappear?
Awakened, they'd regret they've lost a thousand days;
Coming here, they will find the river freely rolls.
If on the riverside rocks you turn your gaze,
You will find only honeycombs of the punt poles.
If your mind from earthly things is detached and freed,
Although nature may change, at ease you will remain.
Let us go back in a boat or on a steed.
Our Abbot will not like such an argument vain.

我生乘化日夜逝，坐觉一念逾新罗。
纷纷争夺醉梦里，岂信荆棘埋铜驼。
觉来俯仰失千劫，回视此水殊委蛇。
君看岸边苍石上，古来篙眼如蜂窠。
但应此心无所住，造物虽驶如余何。
回船上马各归去，多言譊譊师所呵。

Tune: "Joy of Eternal Union"

I lodged at the Pavilion of Swallows in Pencheng, dreamed of the fair lady Panpan and wrote the following lyric.

The bright moonlight is like frost white,
The breeze is cool like waves serene;
Far and wide extends the night scene.
In the haven fish leap
And dewdrops roll down lotus leaves
In solitude no man perceives.
Drums beat thrice in the night so deep,
E'en a leaf falls with sound so loud
That, gloomy, I awake from my dream of the cloud.
Under the boundless pall of night,
Nowhere again can she be found,
Although I've searched o'er the garden's ground.

A tired wanderer far from home
Vainly through mountains and hills may roam;
His native land from view is blocked.
The Pavilion of Swallows is empty. Where
Is the lady Pan-pan so fair?
In the pavilion only swallows' nest is locked.
Both the past and the present are like dreams
From which we have ne'er been awake, it seems.
We've left but pleasures old and sorrows new.
Some future day others will come to view
The Yellow Tower's night scenery;
Would they then sigh for me!

永遇乐

彭城夜宿燕子楼，梦盼盼，因作此词。

明月如霜，好风如水，清景无限。
曲港跳鱼，圆荷泻露，寂寞无人见。
紞如三鼓，铿然一叶，黯黯梦云惊断。
夜茫茫，重寻无处，觉来小园行遍。

天涯倦客，山中归路，望断故园心眼。
燕子楼空，佳人何在，空锁楼中燕。
古今如梦，何曾梦觉，但有旧欢新怨。
异时对，黄楼夜景，为余浩叹。

Tune: "Song of a Fairy in the Cave"

When I was seven, a ninety-year-old nun told me that she had visited the palace of King Meng Chang, where she saw, on a sweltering hot night, the king and his favorite, Lady Pistil, sitting in the shade by a big pool, writing a poem, which she could still recite. Now forty years have passed. As the nun died long ago, nobody knows that poem now. I still remember the first two lines and think it was perhaps written to the tune of the "Song of a Fairy in the Cave." So I complete Meng Chang's poem as follows:*

Your jade-like bones and ice-like skin
Are naturally sweatless, fresh and cool.
The breeze brings unperceivable fragrance in
And fills the bower by the pool.
The broidered screen rolled up lets in
The moon, which peeps at you so fair,
Leaning upon the pillow, not asleep, a pin
Across disheveled hair.

We two rise hand in hand;
Silent in the courtyard we stand.
At times we see shooting stars stray
Across the Milky Way.
How old has night become?
The watchmen thrice have beaten the drum.
The golden moonbeams fade,
Low is the Dipper's string of jade.
We count on fingers when the western wind will blow.
What can we do with years that drift as rivers flow?

---

* See Lady Pistil's poem, "Written at the Capitulation of the Kingdom of Shu."

洞仙歌

余七岁时，见眉州老尼，姓朱，忘其名，年九十岁。自言尝随其师入蜀主孟昶宫中。一日大热，蜀主与花蕊夫人夜纳凉摩诃池上，作一词。朱具能记之。今四十年，朱已死久矣，人无知此词者，但记其首两句，暇日寻味，岂《洞仙歌》令乎？乃为足之云。

冰肌玉骨，自清凉无汗。
水殿风来暗香满。
绣帘开，一点明月窥人，
人未寝，欹枕钗横鬓乱。
起来携素手，庭户无声，时见疏星渡河汉。
试问夜如何？夜已三更，
金波淡，玉绳低转。
但屈指西风几时来，又不道流年暗中偷换。

Tune: "Charm of a Maiden Singer" Memories of the Past at Red Cliff*

The endless river eastward flows;
With its huge waves are gone all those
Gallant heroes of bygone years.
West of the ancient fortress appears
Red Cliff, where General Zhou Yu won his early fame
When the Three Kingdoms were in flame.
Jagged rocks tower in the air
And swashing waves beat on the shore,
Rolling up a thousand heaps of snow.
To match the hills and the river so fair,
How many heroes brave of yore
Made a great show!

I fancy General Zhou Yu at the height
Of his success, with a plume fan in hand,
In a silk hood, so brave and bright,
Laughing and jesting with his bride so fair,
While enemy ships were destroyed as planned
Like castles in the air.
Should their souls revisit this land,
Sentimental, his bride would laugh to say:
Younger than they, I have my hair turned grey.
Life is like a passing dream.
O moon, I drink to you who saw them on the stream.

* Scene of the battle in AD 208 when General Zhou Yu defeated Cao Cao's advancing forces.

念奴娇·赤壁怀古

大江东去，浪淘尽，千古风流人物。
故垒西边，人道是，三国周郎赤壁。
乱石穿空，惊涛拍岸，卷起千堆雪。
江山如画，一时多少豪杰。

遥想公瑾当年，小乔初嫁了，雄姿英发。
羽扇纶巾，谈笑间，樯橹灰飞烟灭。
故国神游，多情应笑我，早生华发。
人生如梦，一樽还酹江月。

Written on the Wall of West Forest Temple*

It's a range viewed in face and peaks viewed from the side,
Assuming different shapes viewed from far and wide.
Of Mount Lu we cannot make out the true face,
For we are lost in the heart of the very place.

* Written when the poet visited Mount Lu in Jiangxi Province.

题西林壁

横看成岭侧成峰，
远近高低各不同。
不识庐山真面目，
只缘身在此山中。

Tune: "Water-dragon Chant"

After Zhang Zhifu's lyric on willow catkins, using the same rhyme scheme.

They seem to be but are not flowers;
None pity them when they fall down in showers.
Forsaking leafy home,
By the roadside they roam.
I think they're fickle, but they've sorrow deep.
Their grief-o'erladen bowels tender,
Like willow branches slender.
And willow leaves like wistful eyes near shut with sleep,
About to open, yet soon closed again.
They dream of drifting with the wind for long,
Long miles to find their men,
But are aroused by orioles' song.

Grieve not for willow catkins flown away,
But that in Western Garden fallen petals red
Can't be restored. When dawns the day
And rain is o'er, we cannot find their traces
But in a pond with duckweeds overspread.*
Of spring's three graces,
Two have gone with the roadside dust
And one with the waves. But if you just
Take a close look, then you will never
Find willow down but tears of those who sever,
Which drop by drop
Fall without stop.

* The poet's own note: it is said that when willow down falls into the water, it turns into duckweed.

水龙吟·次韵章质夫杨花词

似花还似非花，也无人惜从教坠。
抛家傍路，思量却是，无情有思。
萦损柔肠，困酣娇眼，欲开还闭。
梦随风万里，寻郎去处，又还被、莺呼起。

不恨此花飞尽，恨西园、落红难缀。
晓来雨过，遗踪何在？一池萍碎。
春色三分，二分尘土，一分流水。
细看来，不是杨花，点点是离人泪。

LI ZHIYI
(1038-1117)

Tune: "Song of Divination"

I live upstream and you downstream;
From night to night of you I dream.
Unlike the stream, you're not in view,
Though both we drink from River Blue.

When will the river no more flow?
When will my grief no longer grow?
I wish your heart would be like mine,
Then not in vain for you I'd pine.

李之仪
（1038–1117）

卜算子

我住长江头，君住长江尾。
日日思君不见君，共饮长江水。

此水几时休，此恨何时已。
只愿君心似我心，定不负相思意。

HUANG TINGJIAN
(1045-1105)

Tune: "Pure, Serene Music" Late Spring

Away spring goes!
Which way, which way?*
Whoever knows,
Please call her back to stay!

Spring's gone. Towards which land?
Ask orioles, who sing
A hundred tunes none understand.
Riding the wind, they're on the wing.

* This and the following line, Weng Xianliang's translation versified.

黄庭坚
（*1045–1105*）

清平乐·晚春

春归何处？寂寞无行路。
若有人知春去处，唤取归来同住。

春无踪迹谁知？除非问取黄鹂。
百啭无人能解，因风飞过蔷薇。

QIN GUAN
(1049-1100)

Tune: "Courtyard Full of Fragrance"

A belt of clouds girds mountains high
And withered grass spreads to the sky;
The painted horn at the watchtower blows.
Before my boat sails up,
Let's drink a farewell cup.
How many things do I recall in bygone days
All lost in mist and haze!
Beyond the setting sun I see but dots of crows
And that around a lonely village water flows.

I'd call to mind the soul-consuming hour
When I took off your perfume purse unseen
And loosened your silk girdle in your bower.
All this has merely won me in the mansion green*
The title of a fickle lover.
Now I'm a rover,
Oh, when can I see you again?
My tears are shed in vain;
In vain they wet my sleeves.
It grieves
My heart to find your bower out of sight;
It's lost at dusk in city light.

* The mansion where beautiful singing girls lived.

秦观
（1049–1100）

满庭芳

山抹微云，天连衰草，画角声断谯门。
暂停征棹，聊共引离尊。
多少蓬莱旧事，空回首、烟霭纷纷。
斜阳外，寒鸦万点，流水绕孤村。

销魂。当此际，香囊暗解，罗带轻分。
谩赢得、青楼薄幸名存。
此去何时见也，襟袖上、空惹啼痕。
伤情处，高城望断，灯火已黄昏。

Tune: "Immortal at the Magpie Bridge"

Clouds float like works of art;
Stars shoot with grief at heart.
Across the Milky Way the Cowherd meets the Maid.*
When autumn's Golden Wind embraces Dew of Jade,
All the love scenes on earth, however many, fade.

Their tender love flows like a stream;
This happy date seems but a dream.
How can they bear a separate homeward way?
If love between both sides can last for aye,
Why need they stay together night and day?

* According to Chinese legend, the Cowherd and the Maid, or the Weaver, two stars separated by the Milky Way, were to meet across a magpie bridge once every year on the seventh day of the seventh lunar month.

鹊桥仙

纤云弄巧，飞星传恨，银汉迢迢暗度。
金风玉露一相逢，便胜却人间无数。

柔情似水，佳期如梦，忍顾鹊桥归路。
两情若是久长时，又岂在朝朝暮暮。

Tune: "A Riverside Town"

Like northbound swan and southward-flying swallow fleet,
By chance we meet;
Sadly we greet.
We see no more dark hair and beaming face of then
But two old feeble men.
Don't ask about the long, long years since we did part!
Whatever wrings the heart,
Better keep it apart!

Draw from this vat rice wine we made in spring,*
Every drop glistening.
There is no hurry. Fill our golden cup!
Having drunk up,
Like flowers fallen on the stream we go our way.
We'll meet someday,
But who knows where? The misty waves stretch far and nigh,
Cloudy the evening sky.

---

* Weng Xianliang's translation versified.

江城子

南来飞燕北归鸿，偶相逢，惨愁容。
绿鬓朱颜重见两衰翁。
别后悠悠君莫问，无限事，不言中。

小槽春酒滴珠红，莫匆匆，满金钟。
饮散落花流水各西东。
后会不知何处是，烟浪远，暮云重。

HE ZHU
(1052-1125)

Tune: "The Partridge Sky"

All things have changed. Once more I pass the city gate.
We came together; I go back without my mate.
Bitten by hoary frost, half of the plane tree dies;
Lifelong companion lost, one lonely lovebird flies.

Grass wet with dew
Dries on the plain;
How can I leave our old abode and her grave new!
In a half-empty bed I hear the pelting rain.
Who will turn up the wick to mend my coat again?

贺铸
（1052–1125）

鹧鸪天

重过阊门万事非，同来何事不同归。
梧桐半死清霜后，头白鸳鸯失伴飞。

原上草，露初晞。旧栖新垅两依依。
空床卧听南窗雨，谁复挑灯夜补衣。

Tune: "Green-Jade Cup"

Never, never again
Will you tread on the waves along the lakeside lane![*]
I follow with my eyes
The fragrant dusts that rise.
With whom are you now spending your delightful hours,
Playing on zither string,
On a bridge 'neath the moon, in a yard full of flowers,
Or at the curtained window of a crimson bower,
A dwelling only known to spring?

At dusk the floating cloud leaves the grass-fragrant plain;
With blooming brush I write heartbroken verse again.
If you ask me how deep and wide I am lovesick,
Just see the misty stream where weed grows thick,
The town o'erflowed with willow down that wafts on breeze,
The drizzling rain that yellows all mume trees!

---

* The poet lived on the lakeside lane.

青玉案

凌波不过横塘路，但目送、芳尘去。
锦瑟华年谁与度？
月桥花院，琐窗朱户，只有春知处。

飞云冉冉蘅皋暮，彩笔新题断肠句。
试问闲情都几许？
一川烟草，满城风絮，梅子黄时雨。

ZHOU BANGYAN
(1057-1121)

Tune: "Auspicious-Dragon Chant"

Along the street to mansions green*
Some twigs of faded mumes can still be seen
And peach trees try to put forth blossoms sweet.
So quiet are the houses on the street;
The swallows seeking rest
Come back to their old nest.

I stand still, lost in thought of you,
So young, so fond, who came
To peep through cracks between the door and its frame.
At dawn, just thinly powdered in the yellow hue,
Against the wind you tried to hide
Your face in sleeves, giggling aside.

I who once came now come again;
Neighboring houses still remain,
Where I saw you sing and dance then.
Only the Autumn Belle of yore
Enjoys a fair fame as before.

* The mansions where beautiful singing girls lived.

周邦彦
（1057–1121）

瑞龙吟

章台路。还见褪粉梅梢，试花桃树。
愔愔坊陌人家，定巢燕子，归来旧处。
黯凝伫。因念个人痴小，乍窥门户。
侵晨浅约宫黄，障风映袖，盈盈笑语。

前度刘郎重到，访邻寻里，同时歌舞。
唯有旧家秋娘，声价如故。

Trying my pen, I write a poem new.
Can I forget the old one writ for you?
If I but knew
Who is drinking with you in a garden of pleasure,
Or strolling now with you east of the town at leisure!
The past is gone
With lonely swan.
I seek for spring
Only to find past sorrow lingering.
The willows bend with their leaves painted gold;
I come away as it is late and cold.
The poolside drizzle grieves.
Back to the heartbreaking courtyard,
I see scenery willow down weaves
As wind blows hard.

吟笺赋笔，犹记燕台句。
知谁伴、名园露饮，东城闲步。
事与孤鸿去。探春尽是，伤离意绪。
官柳低金缕。归骑晚、纤纤池塘飞雨。
断肠院落，一帘风絮。

Tune: "Wandering of a Youth"*

Southern salt white as snow, northern knife bright as ice,
Her fingers fair a fresh mandarin orange slice.
In the just warmed-up curtained room they are sojourning;
In animal-shaped burner incense ne'er stops burning.
As they sit face to face,
She plays the flute with grace.

To him she whispers low,
"Where will you go?
The watchmen have already gone three rounds.
Horse hoofs may slip on frosty grounds.
You'd better stay.
There are few people on the way."

* The poet was once the rival of Emperor Hui Zong of the Song Dynasty for the love of a famous singing girl, Li Shishi. One night he was with her when the emperor came with a fresh mandarin orange. The poet hid under the bed, heard what they said and wrote this lyric.

少年游

并刀如水，吴盐胜雪，纤手破新橙。
锦幄初温，兽烟不断，相对坐调笙。

低声问：向谁行宿？城上已三更。
马滑霜浓，不如休去，直是少人行。

MOQI YONG
(Dates Unknown)

Tune: "Everlasting Longing"

Watch after watch
And drop by drop,
The rain falls on banana leaves without a stop.
Within the window by the candlelight,
For you I'm longing all the night.

I cannot seek for dreams
Nor banish sorrow.
The rain cares not what I dislike, it seems;
On marble steps it drips until the morrow.

万俟咏
（生卒年不详）

长相思·雨

一声声。一更更。窗外芭蕉窗里灯。
此时无限情。

梦难成。恨难平。不道愁人不喜听。
空阶滴到明。

ZHU DUNRU
(1081-1159)

Tune: "Joy of Meeting"

I lean on western railings on the city wall
Of Jinling* in the fall.
Shedding its rays o'er miles and miles, the sun hangs low
To see the endless river flow.

The Central Plain is in a mess;
Officials scatter in distress.
When to recover our frontiers?
Ask the sad wind to blow over Yangzhou my tears!

* Jinling, present-day Nanjing, was on the southern shore of the Yangtze River and Yangzhou on the northern shore, occupied by the Jurchen invaders.

朱敦儒

（1081–1159）

相见欢

金陵城上西楼，倚清秋。
万里夕阳垂地，大江流。

中原乱，簪缨散，几时收？
试倩悲风吹泪，过扬州。

ZHAO JI
(1082-1135) *

Tune: "Hillside Pavilion" Apricot Seen in the North

Petals on petals of well-cut fine silk ice-white,
Evenly touched with rouge light,
Your fashion new and overflowing charm make shy
All fragrant palace maids on high.
How easy 'tis for you to fade!
You cannot bear the cruel wind and shower's raid on raid.
I'm sad to ask the courtyard sad and drear
How many waning springs have haunted here.

My heart is overladen with deep grief,
How could a pair of swallows give relief?
Could they know what I say?
'Neath boundless sky my ancient palace's far away.
Between us countless streams and mountains stand.
Could swallows find my native land?
Could I forget these mountains and these streams?
But I cannot go back except in dreams.
I know that dreams believed can never be,
But recently e'en dreams would no more come to me!

* Emperor Hui Zong of the Song Dynasty (see Zhou Bangyan's poem), captured by Jurchen invaders and sent to the north as captive.

赵佶
（1082–1135）

燕山亭・北行见杏花

裁剪冰绡，轻叠数重，淡著胭脂匀注。
新样靓妆，艳溢香融，羞杀蕊珠宫女。
易得凋零，更多少、无情风雨。
愁苦。闲院落凄凉，几番春暮。

凭寄离恨重重，这双燕，何曾会人言语。
天遥地远，万水千山，知他故宫何处。
怎不思量，除梦里、有时曾去。
无据，和梦也新来不做。

LI QINGZHAO
(1084-1151)

Tune: "Like a Dream"

Last night the wind was strong and the rain fine;
Sound sleep did not dispel the taste of wine.
I ask the maid who's rolling up the screen.
"The same crab-apple tree," she says, "is seen."
"But don't you know,
But don't you know
The red should languish and the green must grow?"

Tune: "A Twig of Mume Blossoms"

Pink fragrant lotus fade; autumn chills mat of jade,
My silk robe unfastened, I float
Alone in an orchid boat.
Who in the cloud would bring me letters in brocade?
When swans come back in flight,
My bower's steeped in moonlight.
As flowers fall and water carries them away,
One longing overflows
And two places share same woes.
Such sorrow can by no means be driven away;
From eyebrows kept apart,
It now gnaws my heart.

李清照
（1084–1151）

如梦令

昨夜雨疏风骤，浓睡不消残酒。
试问卷帘人，却道海棠依旧。
知否，知否？应是绿肥红瘦。

一剪梅

红藕香残玉簟秋。轻解罗裳，独上兰舟。
云中谁寄锦书来，雁字回时，月满西楼。
花自飘零水自流。一种相思，两处闲愁。
此情无计可消除，才下眉头，却上心头。

Tune: "Tipsy in the Flowers' Shade"

Thin is the mist and thick the clouds, so sad I stay.
From golden censer incense smokes all day.
The Double Ninth* comes now again;
Alone I still remain
In the curtain of gauze, on pillow smooth like jade,
Feeling the midnight chill invade.

At dusk I drink before chrysanthemums in bloom;
My sleeves are filled with fragrance and with gloom.
Say not my soul
Is not consumed. Should western wind uproll
The curtain of my bower,
'Twould show a thinner face than yellow flower.

* On the ninth day of the ninth lunar month the poetess felt her soul consumed by separation from her beloved husband.

醉花阴

薄雾浓云愁永昼，瑞脑销金兽。
佳节又重阳，玉枕纱橱，半夜凉初透。

东篱把酒黄昏后，有暗香盈袖。
莫道不销魂，帘卷西风，人比黄花瘦。

Tune: "Playing Flute Recalled on Phoenix Terrace"

Incense in gold
Censer is cold.
I toss in bed,
Quilt like waves red.
Getting up idly, I won't comb my hair;
My dressing table undusted, I leave it there.
Now the sun seems to hang on the drapery's hook.
I fear the parting grief would make me sadder look.
I've much to say, yet pause as soon as I begin.
Recently I've grown thin,
Not that I'm sick with wine,
Nor that for autumn sad I pine.

Be done! Be done!
Once you are gone,
No matter what parting songs we sing anew,
We can't keep you.
Far, far away you pass your days;
My bower here is drowned in haze.
In front there is a running brook
That could never forget my longing look.
From now on, where
I gaze all day long with a vacant stare,
A new grief will grow there.

凤凰台上忆吹箫

香冷金猊，被翻红浪，起来慵自梳头。
任宝奁尘满，日上帘钩。
生怕离怀别苦，多少事、欲说还休。
新来瘦，非干病酒，不是悲秋。

休休！这回去也，千万遍阳关，也则难留。
念武陵人远，烟锁秦楼。
唯有楼前流水，应念我、终日凝眸。
凝眸处，从今又添，一段新愁。

Tune: "Spring in Peach-Blossom Land"

Sweet flowers fall to dust when winds abate.
Tired, I won't comb my hair although it's late.
Things are the same, but he's no more and all is o'er.
Before I speak, how can my tears not pour!

'Tis said at Twin Creek spring is not yet gone.
In a light boat I long to float thereon.
But I'm afraid the grief-o'erladen boat
Upon Twin Creek can't keep afloat.

武陵春

风住尘香花已尽，日晚倦梳头。
物是人非事事休，欲语泪先流。

闻说双溪春尚好，也拟泛轻舟。
只恐双溪舴艋舟，载不动许多愁。

Tune: "Slow, Slow Song"

I look for what I miss;
I know not what it is.
I feel so sad, so drear,
So lonely, without cheer.
How hard is it
To keep me fit
In this lingering cold!
Hardly warmed up
By cup on cup
Of wine so dry,
Oh, how could I
Endure at dusk the drift
Of wind so swift?
It breaks my heart, alas,
To see the wild geese pass,
For they are my acquaintances of old.

The ground is covered with yellow flowers,
Faded and fallen in showers.
Who will pick them up now?
Sitting alone at the window, how
Could I but quicken
The pack of darkness that won't thicken?
On plane's broad leaves a fine rain drizzles
As twilight grizzles.
Oh, what can I do with a grief
Beyond belief!

声声慢

寻寻觅觅，冷冷清清，凄凄惨惨戚戚。
乍暖还寒时候，最难将息。
三杯两盏淡酒，怎敌他、晚来风急？
雁过也，正伤心，却是旧时相识。

满地黄花堆积。憔悴损，如今有谁堪摘？
守着窗儿，独自怎生得黑？
梧桐更兼细雨，到黄昏、点点滴滴。
这次第，怎一个愁字了得！

LV BENZHONG
(1084-1145)

Tune: "Song of Picking Mulberries"

I'm grieved to find you unlike the moon at its best,
North, south, east, west.
North, south, east, west,
It would accompany me without any rest.

I am grieved to find you like the moon, which would fain
Now wax now wane.
You wax and wane,
When will you come around like the full moon again?

吕本中
（1084–1145）

采桑子

恨君不似江楼月，南北东西。
南北东西，只有相随无别离。

恨君却似江楼月，暂满还亏。
暂满还亏，待得团圆是几时？

CHEN YUYI
(1090-1138)

Tune: "Immortal at the River" Mounting a Tower at Night and Recalling Old Friends Visiting Luoyang Together

I still remember drinking on the Bridge of Noon
With bright wits of the day.
The silent moon
On endless river rolled away.
In lacy shadows cast by apricot flowers
We played the flute till morning hours

O'er twenty years have passed like dreams;
It is a wonder that I'm still alive.
Carefree, I mount the tower bathed in moonbeams.
So many things passed long
Ago survive
Only in fishermen's midnight song.

陈与义

（1090–1138）

临江仙·夜登小阁，忆洛中旧游

忆昔午桥桥上饮，坐中多是豪英。
长沟流月去无声。
杏花疏影里，吹笛到天明。

二十余年如一梦，此身虽在堪惊。
闲登小阁看新晴。
古今多少事，渔唱起三更。

ZHANG YUANGAN
(1091-c. 1170)

Tune: "Congratulations to the Bridegroom" Seeing His Excellence Hu Quan* Banished South

Haunted by dreams of the lost Central Plain,
I hear the autumn wind complain.
From tent to tent horns dreary blow;
In ancient palace weeds o'ergrow.
How could Mount Pillar** suddenly fall down
And Yellow River overflow the town,
A thousand villages overrun with foxes and hares***?
We can't question the heaven high;****
The court will soon forget humiliating affairs.
'Tis sad and drear
To say good-bye
At Southern Pier.

* A high official of the Southern Song Dynasty who was against the capitulatory policy and was banished in 1142 to the southernmost place, where even wild geese carrying messages were not supposed to go.
** Mount Pillar alludes to the royal court.
*** Foxes and hares-the Jurchen aggressors.
****The heaven alludes to the emperor of the Song Dynasty.

张元幹
（1091– 约 1170）

贺新郎 · 送胡邦衡待制赴新州

梦绕神州路。
怅秋风、连营画角，故宫离黍。
底事昆仑倾砥柱，九地黄流乱注。
聚万落千村狐兔。
天意从来高难问，况人情老易悲难诉。
更南浦，送君去。

Cold breath of river willows flies away
The remnant heat of summer day.
The Milky Way slants low;
Past pale moon and sparse stars clouds slowly go.
Mountains and rivers stretch out of view.
Oh, where shall I find you?
I still remember our talking at dead
Of night while we two lay in bed.
But now wild geese can't go so far.
Who will send my letters where you are?
I gaze on azure sky,
Thinking of the hard times gone by.
Can we have but personal love or hate
As beardless young men often state?
Hold up a cup of wine
And hear this song of mine!

凉生岸柳催残暑。
耿斜河，疏星残月，断云微度。
万里江山知何处？回首对床夜语。
雁不到，书成谁与？
目尽青天怀今古，肯儿曹恩怨相尔汝！
举大白，听金缕。

YUE FEI
(1103-1141)

Tune: "The River All Red"

Wrath sets on end my hair;
I lean on railings where
I see the drizzling rain has ceased.
Raising my eyes
Towards the skies,
I heave long sighs,
My wrath not yet appeased.
To dust is gone the fame achieved in thirty years;
Like cloud-veiled moon the thousand-mile land disappears.*
Should youthful heads in vain turn grey,
We would regret for aye.

Lost our capitals,
What a burning shame!
How can we generals
Quench our vengeful flame!
Driving our chariots of war, we'd go
To break through our relentless foe.
Valiantly we'd cut off each head;
Laughing, we'd drink the blood they shed.
When we've reconquered our lost land,
In triumph would return our army grand.

* The Central Plain was occupied by the Jurchen invaders.

岳飞

（1103–1141）

满江红

怒发冲冠，凭栏处、潇潇雨歇。
抬望眼，仰天长啸，壮怀激烈。
三十功名尘与土，八千里路云和月。
莫等闲，白了少年头，空悲切！

靖康耻，犹未雪。臣子恨，何时灭！
驾长车，踏破贺兰山缺。
壮志饥餐胡虏肉，笑谈渴饮匈奴血。
待从头、收拾旧山河，朝天阙。

LU YOU
(1125-1210)

The Storm on the Fourth Day of the Eleventh Lunar Month

Forlorn in a cold bed, I'm grieved not for my plight,
Still thinking of recovering our lost frontiers.
Hearing the stormy wind and rain at dead of night,
I dreamed of frozen rivers crossed by cavaliers.

Testament to My Son

After my death I know for me all hopes are vain,
But still I'm grieved to see our country not unite.
When royal armies recover the Central Plain,
Do not forget to tell your sire in sacred rite!

陆游
（1125–1210）

十一月四日风雨大作

僵卧孤村不自哀，尚思为国戍轮台。
夜阑卧听风吹雨，铁马冰河入梦来。

示儿

死去元知万事空，但悲不见九州同。
王师北定中原日，家祭无忘告乃翁。

The Garden of Shen* (I)

Your fragrance has not sweetened my dreams for forty years;
The willows grow so old that no catkin appears.
I'll soon become a clod of clay beneath the hill;
Though drowned in tears, I come to find your traces still.

The Garden of Shen (II)

The horn blows sad at sunset on the city wall;
In garden of old days I find no poolside hall.
To see green waves beneath the bridge would break my heart,
For they have seen your swanlike shadow come and part.

* In the Garden of Shen the poet met his first wife, Tang Wan, whom he loved dearly, yet was compelled to divorce. They wrote two lyrics to the tune of "Phoenix Hairpin" in 1155. In 1200 the poet revisited the garden alone and wrote these two poems.

沈园二首（其一）

梦断香消四十年，沈园柳老不吹绵。
此身行作稽山土，犹吊遗踪一泫然。

沈园二首（其二）

城上斜阳画角哀，沈园非复旧池台，
伤心桥下春波绿，曾是惊鸿照影来。

Tune: "Phoenix Hairpin"[*]

Pink hands so fine,
Gold-branded wine,[**]
Spring paints green willows palace walls cannot confine.
East wind unfair,
Happy times rare.
In my heart sad thoughts throng;
We've severed for years long.
Wrong, wrong, wrong!

Spring is as green,
In vain she's lean,
Her silk scarf soaked with tears and red with stains unclean.
Peach blossoms fall
Near deserted hall.
Our oath is still there. Lo!
No word to her can go.
No, no, no!

* See Lu You's poem "The Garden of Shen."
** The wine offered to the poet by his first wife, Tang Wan.

钗头凤

红酥手，黄縢酒，满城春色宫墙柳。
东风恶，欢情薄。
一怀愁绪，几年离索。错，错，错。

春如旧，人空瘦，泪痕红浥鲛绡透。
桃花落，闲池阁。
山盟虽在，锦书难托。莫，莫，莫！

TANG WAN
(1128 -1156)

Tune: "Phoenix Hairpin"*

The world unfair,
True manhood rare.
Dusk melts away in rain and blooming trees turn bare.
Morning wind high,
Tear traces dry.
I'll write to you what's in my heart,
Leaning on rails, speaking apart.
Hard, hard, hard!

Go each our ways!
Gone are our days.
Like long, long ropes of swing my sick soul groans always.
The horn blows cold,
Night has grown old.
Afraid my grief may be descried,
I try to hide my tears undried.
Hide, hide, hide!

* See Lu You's poem "The Garden of Shen."

唐婉

（*1128–1156*）

钗头凤

世情薄，人情恶，雨送黄昏花易落。
晓风干，泪痕残。
欲笺心事，独语斜阑。难，难，难！

人成各，今非昨，病魂常似秋千索。
角声寒，夜阑珊。
怕人寻问，咽泪装欢。瞒，瞒，瞒！

YANG WANLI
(1127-1206)

The West Lake

The uncommon West Lake in the midst of sixth moon
Displays a scenery to other months unknown:
Green lotus leaves outspread as far as boundless sky
Pink lotus blossoms take from sunshine a new dye.

杨万里

（1127–1206）

晓出净慈寺送林子方

毕竟西湖六月中，
风光不与四时同。
接天莲叶无穷碧，
映日荷花别样红。

ZHU XI
(1130-1200)

The Book*

There lies a glassy oblong pool,
Where light and shade pursue their course.
How can it be so clear and cool?
For water fresh comes from its source.

* The book is compared to a clear pool.

朱熹
（1130–1200）

观书有感

半亩方塘一鉴开，
天光云影共徘徊。
问渠那得清如许？
为有源头活水来。

ZHANG XIAOXIANG
(1132-1169)

Tune: "The Charm of a Maiden Singer" Passing Lake Dongting

Lake Dongting, Lake Green Grass,
Near the Midautumn night,
Unruffled for no winds pass,
Like thirty thousand acres of jade bright
Dotted with the leaflike boat of mine.
The skies with pure moonbeams o'erflow;
The water surface paved with moonshine:
Brightness above, brightness below.
My heart with the moon becomes one,
Felicity to share with none.

Thinking of the southwest, where I passed a year,
To lonely pure moonlight akin,
I feel my heart and soul snow and ice clear.
Although my hair is short and sparse, my gown too thin
In the immense expanse I keep floating up.
Drinking wine from the River West
And using Dipper as wine cup,
I invite Nature to be my guest.
Beating time aboard and crooning alone,
I sink deep into time and place unknown.

张孝祥

（1132–1169）

念奴娇 · 过洞庭

洞庭青草，近中秋，更无一点风色。
玉界琼田三万顷，着我扁舟一叶。
素月分辉，明河共影，表里俱澄澈。
悠然心会，妙处难与君说。

应念岭表经年，孤光自照，肝胆皆冰雪。
短发萧骚襟袖冷，稳泛沧浪空阔。
尽挹西江，细斟北斗，万象为宾客。
扣舷独啸，不知今夕何夕。

XIN QiJI
(1140-1207)

Tune: "Groping for Fish"

In 1179, before I was transferred from Hubei to Hunan, Wang Zheng-zhi, a colleague of mine, feasted me in the Little Hill Pavilion and I wrote the following.

How much more can spring bear of wind and rain?
Too hastily 'twill leave again.
Lovers of spring would fear to see the flowers red
Budding too soon and fallen petals too widespread.
O spring, please stay!
I've heard it said that sweet grass far away
Would stop you from seeing your return way.
But I've not heard
Spring say a word;
Only the busy spiders weave
Webs all day by the painted cave
To keep the willow down from taking leave.

辛弃疾

（1140–1207）

摸鱼儿

淳熙己亥，自湖北漕移湖南，同官王正之置酒小山亭，为赋。

更能消几番风雨？匆匆春又归去。
惜春长怕花开早，何况落红无数。
春且住，见说道、天涯芳草无归路。
怨春不语。
算只有殷勤，画檐蛛网，尽日惹飞絮。

Could a disfavored consort again to favor rise?
Could beauty not be envied by green eyes?
Even if favor could be bought back again,
To whom of this unrequited love can she complain?
Do not dance, then!
Have you not seen
Both plump and slender beauties turn to dust?
Bitterest grief is just
That you can't do
What you want to.
Oh, do not lean
On overhanging rails where the setting sun sees
Heartbroken willow trees!*

* In the first stanza the poet sighed for the departing spring, for he and Wang could not do what they wanted, that is, drive away Jurchen invaders from the occupied territory. In the second stanza he compared Wang to a disfavored beauty and the capitulators to plump and slender dancers in favor. The willow trees were heartbroken, for they saw the sun on the decline.

长门事，准拟佳期又误。蛾眉曾有人妒。
千金纵买相如赋，脉脉此情谁诉？
君莫舞，君不见、玉环飞燕皆尘土！
闲愁最苦！
休去倚危栏，斜阳正在，烟柳断肠处。

Tune: "Slow Song of Zhu Yingtai" Late Spring

E'er since we parted
At Ferry of Peach Leaf,
The willow-darkened southern bank's been drowned in grief.
I dread to go upstairs again;
Nine days in ten are filled with wind and rain.
So, brokenhearted,
I see red petals fall one by one,
Uncared for, and there's none
To plead with orioles singing all the day long
To still their song.

Peering at flowered hairpin on my head,
I take it down to count the petals red
So that I may anticipate
Your returning date,
Till lamplight flickers on my curtained bed.
Words choked in my dream upon
My lips: "Oh, grief has come with spring! I say,
Now spring is gone,
Why won't it carry grief away?"

祝英台近・晚春

宝钗分，桃叶渡，烟柳暗南浦。
怕上层楼，十日九风雨。
断肠片片飞红，都无人管，
更谁劝啼莺声住？

鬓边觑，试把花卜归期，才簪又重数。
罗帐灯昏，哽咽梦中语：
是他春带愁来，春归何处？
却不解、带将愁去。

Tune: "Congratulations to the Bridegroom"*

That I should have aged so!
And my fellows, alas! How many still remain?
Life spent with naught to show
But hair turned silvery in vain.
Yet with a smile I part
With all that is mundane,
Whereof nothing gladdens the heart.
Charming are mountains green.
I would expect the feeling to be
Mutual, for we
Are somewhat alike, in mood and mien.

As I sit at the east window, goblet in hand,
My thoughts go to that poet of Peach-Blossom Land**
Who bemoaned scattered friends and louring cloud.
He was the philosophic drinker true,
Unlike those who
Of fickle fame felt proud.
I turn back crying;
An angry blast be raised and dark clouds flying!
It matters little I can't see the men of old;
Rather a pity they cannot see me!
But even my contemporaries, all told,
How many of them really know me?
But two or three.

---

* Weng Xianliang's translation versified.
**See Tao Qian's poem "Return to Nature."

贺新郎

邑中园亭，仆皆为赋此词。一日，独坐停云，水声山色，竞来相娱。意溪山欲援例者，遂作数语，庶几仿佛渊明思亲友之意云。

甚矣吾衰矣！
怅平生、交游零落，只今余几！
白发空垂三千丈，一笑人间万事。
问何物、能令公喜？
我见青山多妩媚，料青山见我应如是。
情与貌，略相似。

一尊搔首东窗里。
想渊明停云诗就，此时风味。
江左沉酣求名者，岂识浊醪妙理。
回首叫、云飞风起。
不恨古人吾不见，恨古人不见吾狂耳。
知我者，二三子。

Tune: "The Partridge Sky"

As a friend of mine talked about the victory we had won while young, I recollected those bygone days and wrote the following random lyric.

While young, beneath my flag I had ten thousand knights;
With these outfitted cavaliers I crossed the river.
The foe prepared their silver shafts during the nights;
During the days we shot arrows from golden quiver.

Recalling days gone by,
I sigh over my plight;
The vernal wind can't change my hair to black from white.
Since thwarted is my plan for gaining the lost land,
I'd learn from neighbors how to plant fruit trees by hand.

鹧鸪天

有客慨然谈功名，因追念少年时事，戏作。

壮岁旌旗拥万夫，锦襜突骑渡江初。
燕兵夜娖银胡䩮，汉箭朝飞金仆姑。

追往事，叹今吾，春风不染白髭须。
却将万字平戎策，换得东家种树书。

Tune: "Spring in Peach-Blossom Land"* Home Coming

"Just a round trip of three hundred li.
Be back in five days," you told me.
Now I'm one day overdue,
Which must mean long hours of anxiety for you.

"Giddap!" My galloping horse seems too slow,
For impatient I grow.
I shout to a passing magpie,
"Go quick! Tell her I'm coming. Fly!"

* Weng Xianliang's translation versified.

武陵春

走去走来三百里，五日以为期。
六日归时已是疑。应是望多时。

鞭个马儿归去也，心急马行迟。
不免相烦喜鹊儿。先报那人知。

CHEN LIANG
(1143-1194)

Tune: "Prelude to Water Melody" Farewell to Zhang Demao,* Envoy to the Jurchen Aggressors

Not seeing southern troops for long,
Don't say their northern steeds can't run.
Single-handed, at once the thing is done;
After all, we are heroes millions strong.
His Majesty's envoy - what fun!
Should eastward go like overbrimming river
That eastward flows forever.
We bend to the Jurchen tents now;
Another day to us they'll bow.

In the capital of our emperors
And the land of great, long
Empire built by our ancestors,
Is there none who thinks it wrong
To submit to the foe
Whose stink of lamb spreads for miles and miles?
Where's the spirit of heroes who died long ago?
When will our army beat the Jurchen ranks and files?
Why ask about the enemy's fate?
The sun** will surely radiate.

---

* Zhang Demao was the envoy of the southern court, sent alone to bow to the Jurchen chieftain, who was accustomed to eating lamb.
** The Song Empire.

陈亮

（1143–1194）

水调歌头·送章德茂大卿使虏

不见南师久，漫说北群空。
当场只手，毕竟还我万夫雄。
自笑堂堂汉使，得似洋洋河水，
依旧只流东？
且复穹庐拜，会向藁街逢！

尧之都，舜之壤，禹之封。
于中应有，一个半个耻臣戎！
万里腥膻如许，千古英灵安在，
磅礴几时通？
胡运何须问，赫日自当中！

LIU GUO
(1154-1206)

Tune: "The Moon Over the West River"*

Ministers in the court plan the campaign;
Generals, spear in hand, guard the frontier.
When can we take back the lost Central Plain?
Our men, united, should start now and here.

Holding the premiership today,
You'll win high honor tomorrow.
The capital retaken, you may sing the lay
Of "Big Wind"** and people will follow.

* This lyric was written for Premier Han, who planned a northern campaign to take back the lost Central Plain and the lost capital.
** See Liu Bang's "Song of the Big Wind."

刘过
（*1154–1206*）

西江月

堂上谋臣帷幄，边头猛将干戈。
天时地利与人和，“燕可伐欤？”曰：“可。”

此日楼台鼎鼐，他时剑履山河。
都人齐和大风歌，管领群臣来贺。

JIANG KUI
(1155-1221)

Tune: "The Partridge Sky" A Dream on the Night of Lantern Festival*

The endless River Fei to the east keeps on flowing;
The love seed we once sowed forever keeps on growing.
Your face I saw in dream was not clear to my eyes
As in your portrait; soon I'm awakened by birds' cries.

Spring not yet green,
My grey hair seen,
Our separation's been too long to grieve the heart.
Why make the past reappear
Before us from year to year
On Lantern Festival when we are far apart?

* On the fifteenth day of the first lunar month in 1197 the over-forty-year-old poet dreamed of his beloved, from whom he had been separated for over twenty years.

姜夔

（1155–1221）

鹧鸪天·元夕有所梦

肥水东流无尽期。当初不合种相思。
梦中未比丹青见，暗里忽惊山鸟啼。

春未绿，鬓先丝。人间别久不成悲。
谁教岁岁红莲夜，两处沉吟各自知。

YE SHAOWENG
(Dates Unknown)

Calling on a Friend without Meeting Him

How could the green moss like the sabots, whose teeth* sting?
I tap long at the door, but none opens at my call.
The garden can't confine the full beauty of spring;
An apricot extends a blooming branch o'er the wall.

* Chinese sabots had teeth.

叶绍翁
（生卒年不详）

游园不值

应怜屐齿印苍苔，
小扣柴扉久不开。
春色满园关不住，
一枝红杏出墙来。

SHI DAZU
(1163-1220)

Tune: "A Pair of Swallows"

Spring's growing old.
Between the curtain and the screen
The dust in last year's nest is cold.
A pair of swallows bank and halt to see
If they can perch there side by side.
Looking at painted ceiling and carved beams
And twittering, they can't decide,
It seems.
Clipping the tips of blooming tree,
They shed
The shadow of their forked tails so green
And cleave their way through flowers red.

Along the fragrant way
Where rain has wetted clods of clay
They like to skim over the ground,
Striving to be fleet
In flight.
Returning late to mansion sweet,
They've gazed their fill, till in twilight
Dim willows are drowned
And flowers fall asleep.
Now they'd be perching deep
In fragrant nest,
Forgetting to bring message from the end of sky.
Grieved, with eyebrows knit, the lady's seen to rest
Her elbow on the painted rafts and sigh.

史达祖

（1163–1220）

双双燕·咏燕

过春社了，度帘幕中间，去年尘冷。
差池欲住，试入旧巢相并。
还相雕梁藻井。又软语、商量不定。
飘然快拂花梢，翠尾分开红影。

芳径。芹泥雨润。爱贴地争飞，竞夸轻俊。
红楼归晚，看足柳昏花暝。
应自栖香正稳。便忘了、天涯芳信。
愁损翠黛双蛾，日日画阑独凭。

LIU KEZHUANG (1187-1269)

Tune: "Spring in the Garden of Qin" Dreaming of a Deceased Friend*

Again we meet
In wineshop of the north**
And in Bronze Bird Tower. Let the cook make mincemeat
Of the whale caught in eastern sea
And stablemen bring forth
The fiery western steeds for you and me.
Heroes there are in this world: you and I.
Who deserves drinking in our company?
But I will call
Warriors and swordsmen who are not afraid to die.

Let the drums roll! And drink, drink deep!
But down to earth again. The rooster wakes me from sleep.
So it's not to be, after all.
Great deeds might have been, had chance come my way.
It's too late now, I've lost my day.
Even a hero can win honors high
Only under a heroic sage.
Up! Let no future be o'ershadowed by
A nonheroic age!

* Weng Xianliang's translation versified.
** The north was occupied by Jurchen invaders.

刘克庄

（1187–1269）

沁园春·梦孚若

何处相逢，登宝钗楼，访铜雀台。
唤厨人斫就，东溟鲸脍，
圉人呈罢，西极龙媒。
天下英雄，使君与操，
余子谁堪共酒杯。
车千乘，载燕南赵北，剑客奇才。

饮酣画鼓如雷。谁信被晨鸡轻唤回。
叹年光过尽，功名未立，
书生老去，机会方来。
使李将军，遇高皇帝，
万户侯何足道哉。
披衣起，但凄凉感旧，慷慨生哀。

WU WENYING (1200-1260)

Tune: "Wind through Pines"

Hearing the wind and rain while mourning for the dead,*
Sadly I draft an elegy on flowers.
We parted on the dark-green road before these bowers,
Where willow branches hang like thread,
Each inch revealing
Our tender feeling.
I drown my grief in wine in chilly spring;
Drowsy, I wake again when orioles sing.

In Garden West I sweep the pathway
From day to day,
Enjoying the fine view
Still without you.
On the ropes of the swing the wasps often alight
For fragrance spread by fingers fair.
I'm grieved not to see your foot traces; all night
The mossy steps are left untrodden there.

* Chinese people mourned for the dead on the eighth day of the third lunar month.

吴文英

（*1200–1260*）

风入松

听风听雨过清明，愁草瘗花铭。
楼前绿暗分携路，一丝柳、一寸柔情。
料峭春寒中酒，交加晓梦啼莺。

西园日日扫林亭，依旧赏新晴。
黄蜂频扑秋千索，有当时、纤手香凝。
惆怅双鸳不到，幽阶一夜苔生。

LIU CHENWENG (1231-1294)

Tune: "Green Tip of Willow Branch"

Tatar steeds in blankets clad,
Tears shed from lanterns* 'neath the moon,
Spring has come to a town so sad.
The flutes playing a foreign tune
And foreign drumbeats in the street
Can never be called music sweet.

How can I bear to sit alone by dim lamplight,
Thinking of northern land now lost to sight
With palaces steeped in moonlight,
Of southern capital in days gone by,
Of my secluded life in mountains high,
Of grief of those who seaward fly**!

* Lantern Festival in Lin'an (present-day Hangzhou), capital of the Southern Song, occupied by the Tatars in 1276.

** The remnants of unyielding Song forces still carrying on armed resistance on the sea.

刘辰翁
（*1231–1294*）

柳梢青·春感

铁马蒙毡，银花洒泪，春入愁城。
笛里番腔，街头戏鼓，不是歌声。

那堪独坐青灯。想故国、高台月明。
辇下风光，山中岁月，海上心情。

WEN TIANXIANG*
(1236-1282)

Sailing on Lonely Ocean

Delving in the Book of Change, I rose through hardships great
And desperately fought the foe for four long years.
Like willow down the war-torn land looks desolate;
I sink or swim as duckweed in the rain appears.
For perils on Perilous Beach I heaved sighs;
On Lonely Ocean now I feel dreary and lonely.
Since olden days there's never been a man but dies;
I'd leave a loyalist's name in history only.

* Wen Tianxiang passed the civil service examinations with highest honors in 1256 and was appointed prime minister in the court of the Song Dynasty. In 1275 he led the royalist army against the Tatar invaders. Defeated, he passed Perilous Beach in 1276. Captured in 1278, he passed Lonely Ocean, a part of the South China Sea.

文天祥

（1236–1282）

过零丁洋

辛苦遭逢起一经，干戈寥落四周星。
山河破碎风飘絮，身世浮沉雨打萍。
惶恐滩头说惶恐，零丁洋里叹零丁。
人生自古谁无死？留取丹心照汗青！

JIANG JIE
(Dates Unknown)

Tune: "A Twig of Mume Blossoms"

Can boundless vernal grief be drowned in vernal wine?
On waves is tossed my boat;
Before wineshop flags float.
The farewell ferry and the bridge again I pass
When sadly blows the breeze
And rain falls without cease.

When may I go home to wash this outworn robe of mine,
To play on silver flute
And burn the incense mute?
Time and tide will never wait for man, alas!
Cherries red are seen
And bananas green.

蒋捷

（生卒年不详）

一剪梅·舟过吴江

一片春愁待酒浇。江上舟摇，楼上帘招。
秋娘渡与泰娘桥，风又飘飘，雨又萧萧。

何日归家洗客袍？银字笙调，心字香烧。
流光容易把人抛，红了樱桃，绿了芭蕉。

ZHANG YAN
(1248-1320)

Tune: "Ganzhou"

In 1291 Sheng Yao-dao and I came back from the north and then we went separately to Yuezhou and Hangzhou. The next year he came to see me and stayed with me for a few days before parting again. I wrote the following to mark the meeting.

I still remember at the Gate of Jade
A pleasure trip in snow was made.
Our sable coats were stiffened in cold air.
Treading on ancient road by forest bare
Or watering the steeds in endless stream,
We felt relieved as if past grief were but a dream.
But now awake, still on the southern shore I stand,
Shedding tears for my friend in western land.
No verse is written on the fallen leaf,
But still it feels unwritten grief.

You're carried back by a white cloud.
For whom should pendants tinkle loud?
Looking at shadows, who could still feel proud?
Breaking off flower reeds, I would send them afar,
But I'm saddened by autumn as they are.
As usual 'neath the bridge water runs by the shore,
But the gulls standing on the sand aren't those of yore.
In vain I sigh;
At sunset I'm afraid to climb up high.

张炎

（1248–1320）

八声甘州·记玉关踏雪事清游

辛卯岁，沈尧道同余北归，各处杭、越。逾岁，尧道来问寂寞，语笑数日。又复别去。赋此曲，并寄赵学舟。

记玉关踏雪事清游，寒气脆貂裘。
傍枯林古道，长河饮马，此意悠悠。
短梦依然江表，老泪洒西州。
一字无题处，落叶都愁。

载取白云归去，问谁留楚佩，弄影中洲？
折芦花赠远，零落一身秋。
向寻常、野桥流水，待招来，不是旧沙鸥。
空怀感，有斜阳处，却怕登楼。

NIE SHENGQIONG*
(Dates Unknown)

Tune: "The Partridge Sky"**

I see you leave town, jade-pale and sad like a flower;
The willows look so green below the Lotus Tower.
Before a cup of wine I sing a farewell song;
At the fifth post I see you off on journey long.

I seek again
Sweet dreams in vain.
Who knows how deep is my sorrow?
My teardrops on the pillow
And raindrops on the willow
Drip within and without the window till the morrow.

* A singing girl in Chang'an (present-day Xi'an).
** The farewell song she sang to her beloved.

聂胜琼
（生卒年不详）

鹧鸪天·寄李之问

玉惨花愁出凤城，莲花楼下柳青青。
尊前一唱阳关曲，别个人人第五程。

寻好梦，梦难成。有谁知我此时情？
枕前泪共阶前雨，隔个窗儿滴到明。

YUAN DYNASTY

(1271-1368)

元朝

（1271—1368）

ZENG YUNYUAN
(Dates Unknown)

Tune: "Rouged Lips"

The east wind blows all night;
My pillow laden with grief cannot be made light.
The cries of birds wake me from dreams;
I find my window bathed in sunny beams.

You came with spring
And go when spring is aging.
The same green grass
Along the road beneath our feet
Only when you come back, alas,
Will become sweet.

曾允元
（生卒年不详）

点绛唇

一夜东风，枕边吹散愁多少。
数声啼鸟。梦转纱窗晓。

来是春初，去是春将老。
长亭道。一般芳草。只有归时好。

MA ZHIYUAN
(1260-1334)

Autumn–to the Tune of "Clear Sky over the Sand"

O'er old trees wreathed with rotten vine fly evening crows;
'Neath tiny bridge beside a cot a clear stream flows;
On ancient road in western breeze a lean horse goes.
Westward declines the sun;
Far, far from home is the heartbroken one.

马致远

（*1260–1334*）

天净沙·秋思

枯藤老树昏鸦，小桥流水人家，
古道西风瘦马。
夕阳西下，断肠人在天涯。

GUAN HANQING
(c. 1220-c. 1300)

Separation – to the Tune of "Four Pieces of Jade"

When you are gone,
For you I long.
When will my yearning come to an end?
I lean on rails, caressed by snowy willow down.
The stream you went along
At hillside takes a bend.
It's screened from view,
Oh, together with you.

关汉卿

（约 1220– 约 1300）

四块玉·别情

自送别，心难舍，一点相思几时绝？
凭阑袖拂杨花雪。
溪又斜，山又遮，人去也！

WANG SHIFU
(1260-1336)

Parting–to the Tune of "Calm Dignity"*

With clouds the sky turns grey
O'er yellow blooms-paved way.
How bitter blows the western breeze!
From north to south fly all wild geese.
Why like wine-flushed face is frosted forest red?
It's dyed in tears the parting lovers shed.

* From "Romance of the Western Chamber," IV, iii.

王实甫

（1260–1336）

端正好

碧云天，黄花地，
西风紧，北雁南飞。
晓来谁染霜林醉，
总是离人泪。

ZHANG KEJIU
(1270-c. 1349)

Hermitage–to the Tune of "Song of Clear River" *

My sanctuary right in front of mountains proud.
The only intruder's the cloud.
How green the pines surging and singing in the breeze!
How bright the tripod flames licking leaves of oak trees!
A jug of wine and then sleep still.
Oh, let spring go by as it will.

* Weng Xianliang's translation versified.

张可久

（1270– 约 1349）

清江引 · 山居春枕

门前好山云占了，尽日无人到。
松风响翠涛，槲叶烧丹灶。
先生醉眠春自老。

QIAO JI
(1280-1345)

On My Way to Jinlin–to the Tune of "Leaning on the Railings"*

On poetry-burdened jade far, far have I strayed.
The weary birds are wailing o'er huts on my way.
See how the willows shed their catkins at my head
As if it were not touched already with grey!

* Weng Xianliang's translation versified.

乔吉

（*1280–1345*）

凭阑人·金陵道中

瘦马驮诗天一涯，
倦鸟呼愁村数家。
扑头飞柳花，
与人添鬓华。

MING DYNASTY

(1368-1644)

明朝

(1368—1644)

QI JIGUANG*
(1528-1587)

March at Dawn

Our banners undulate along the winding stream
Without disturbing the riverside bird from its dream,
Suddenly we beat drums and blow our bugles shrill
Which startle even the deaf old monk beyond the hill.

* A General and national hero in charge of national defense who had won many victories against Japanese aggressors.

戚继光

（1528–1587）

晓征

霜溪曲曲转旌旗，
几许沙鸥睡未知。
笳鼓声高寒吹起，
深山惊杀老阇黎。

TANG XIANZU
(Dates Unknown)

Excerpts from "The Peony Pavilion"

A riot of deep purple and bright red.
What pity on the ruins they overspread!
Why does Heaven give us brilliant day and dazzling sight?
Whose house could boast of a sweeter delight?
At dawn on high rainbow clouds fly;
At dusk the green pavilion's seen.
In misty waves mingle the threads of rain;
The wind swells sails of painted boats in vain.
For those behind the screens
Make light of vernal scenes.

汤显祖
（生卒年不详）

牡丹亭（选段）

原来姹紫嫣红开遍，
似这般都付与断井颓垣。
良辰美景奈何天，赏心乐事谁家院！
朝飞暮卷，云霞翠轩，
雨丝风片，烟波画船，
锦屏人忒看的这韶光贱。

QING DYNASTY

(1644-1911)

清朝

(1644—1911)

WU WEIYE
(1609-1671)

Song of the Beautiful Yuanyuan

The emperor left the human world on a gloomy day;
The general* to the imperial palace fought his way.
The royal armies dressed in mourning shed their tears;
The wrathful general for his lady wielded his spears.

"Not that I love my lady captured by the foe,
But that I hate to death the rebels spreading woe.
Like lightning sweeping them away at Mountain Black,
O'er father's death I'll weep and bring my lady back."

Remember their first meeting in a nobleman's bower:
She sang and danced as beautifully as a flower.
The nobleman promised to bestow the songstress fair
On General Wu, who carried her home in sedan chair.

Born near the Flower-Washing Stream, she was a maid
Named Yuan-yuan, whose charm outshone silk and brocade.
She dreamed of roving in the royal garden where
She met the king surrounded by his maidens fair.
In previous life he must have been the Fairy Queen;
Before her door there stretched a sea of water green.

---

* General Wu, whose favorite lady Yuanyuan was captured by the peasant army, led the Qing forces in recapturing her in 1644 resulting in the downfall of the Ming Dynasty.

吴伟业
（1609–1671）

圆圆曲

鼎湖当日弃人间，破敌收京下玉关。
恸哭六军俱缟素，冲冠一怒为红颜。

红颜流落非吾恋，逆贼天亡自荒宴。
电扫黄巾定黑山，哭罢君亲再相见。

相见初经田窦家，侯门歌舞出如花。
许将戚里箜篌伎，等取将军油壁车。

家本姑苏浣花里，圆圆小字娇罗绮。
梦向夫差苑里游，宫娥拥入君王起。
前身合是采莲人，门前一片横塘水。

On water green two oars propelled a boat in flight:
A nobleman had carried her away by might.
Who knows on such occasion what her fate would be?
Her tear-soaked robe was all that one could see.

Her bitterness ascended to the skies.
But no one pitied her pearly teeth, her crystal eyes.
She was ravished and shut up inside all day long,
Where she was taught to sing every ravishing song.

The general came and drank his fill till sunset.
To whom could she complain and sing her deep regret?
With our young general bright no gallant could ever vie:
While plucking flowers sweet he often turned his eye.

He freed the singing bird caged behind stout bars.
How many times they crossed the Stream of Silver Stars!
But military orders commanded him to fight;
He promised to be back and left her in sad plight.

How deep his love for her! How hard again to meet
When rebels trampled the capital beneath their feet!
Alas! the lovesick mistress in the tower high
Was taken like the willow catkin in the sky.
Her inner chamber was surrounded all about;
From the carved balustrade she was compelled to come out.
Had not our general beaten the rebel force,
How could his lady fair be rescued on a horse?

The lady on a horse was summoned to appear,
Her hair like tousled cloud, unrecovered from fear.
Two giant candles lit her to the battlefield;
Her pretty face was clouded behind a veil of tears congealed.

横塘双桨去如飞，何处豪家强载归。
此际岂知非薄命，此时唯有泪沾衣。

薰天意气连宫掖，明眸皓齿无人惜。
夺归永巷闭良家，教就新声倾坐客。

坐客飞觞红日暮，一曲哀弦向谁诉？
白皙通侯最少年，拣取花枝屡回顾。

早携娇鸟出樊笼，待得银河几时渡？
恨杀军书抵死催，苦留后约将人误。

相约恩深相见难，一朝蚁贼满长安。
可怜思妇楼头柳，认作天边粉絮看。
遍索绿珠围内第，强呼绛树出雕阑。
若非壮士全师胜，争得蛾眉匹马还？

蛾眉马上传呼进，云鬟不整惊魂定。
蜡炬迎来在战场，啼妆满面残红印。

The general's force, while beating drums, marched its way;
A thousand chariots drove southwest without delay.
In cloud-veiled valley rose a painted tower high;
The setting moon became a mirror to her eye.

To her homeland by riverside the news soon spread
Though ten times maples bitten by frost had turned red.
The master who taught her to sing felt fortunate;
The washerwomen still remembered their lucky mate.

"We're swallows pecking clods of clay to build our nest;
One flying up the tree becomes a phoenix blest.
Before a cup of wine we grieve that old we've grown;
We're glad she's married General Wu who wears a crown."

The lady then felt compromised by far-flung fame:
Her beauty earned for her all noblemen's acclaim.
One casket of bright pearls brought ten caskets of grief:
Her slender waist now wafted for miles like a leaf.
Blame not the breeze that blows down flowers far and nigh!
For boundless spring has come from the earth and sky.

A peerless beauty brings countries up and down
And earns for a gallant hero his lasting renown.
How could a woman care about the state affair?
How could our general forsake his lady fair?
His family slain and turned to dust and clay;
Her rosy dress will shine in history for aye.

专征萧鼓向秦川，金牛道上车千乘。
斜谷云深起画楼，散关月落开妆镜。

传来消息满江乡，乌桕红经十度霜。
教曲伎师怜尚在，浣纱女伴忆同行。

旧巢共是衔泥燕，飞上枝头变凤凰。
长向尊前悲老大，有人夫婿擅侯王。

当时只受声名累，贵戚名豪竞延致。
一斛明珠万斛愁，关山漂泊腰肢细。
错怨狂风飏落花，无边春色来天地。

尝闻倾国与倾城，翻使周郎受重名。
妻子岂应关大计，英雄无奈是多情。
全家白骨成灰土，一代红妆照汗青。

Have you not seen
In Golden Palace where the lovebirds passed the night
The lady was too lovely to be kept out of sight?
On dusty fragrant path now only cries blackbird,
No beauty's steps are heard
Where moss in vain grows green.

Birds' feathers plucked and palace moved, for miles grief reigns:
Pearly teeth sing and green sleeves dance on western plains.
For the conquered Southern Land I sing another song;
But River Han still southeastward flows all day long.

君不见，馆娃初起鸳鸯宿，越女如花看不足。
香径尘生乌自啼，屧廊人去苔空绿。

换羽移宫万里愁，珠歌翠舞古梁州。
为君别唱吴宫曲，汉水东南日夜流！

NALAN XINGDE (1655-1685)

To the Tune of "Song of the Golden Thread"*

Why aggravate our misery?
Let gods do what they will.
Adamant we are; unsullied we shall be.
Life is less full of good than ill.
How many ancients did complain?
Justice is often denied to the intelligent.
Lying alone on a rude couch, I gaze at the Wain;
On city wall a flute is wailing a deep lament.
I hear the drum on the watchtower
Boom out the hour:
The darkest night
Is at its height.

Whoever would be a man
Should seek no patronage;
Better get ready a boat while we can
That we may on five lakes find anchorage.
Useless to staunch my tears copious as autumn rain.
Who would take notice but butterflies on the plain?
I do not envy those at court
Whose dizzy whirl is short.
I let the west wind blow
In capital and chill the moonlight waste!
The cloistered flowers are chaste
As virgin snow.

* Weng Xianliang's translation versified.

纳兰性德

（*1655–1685*）

金缕曲·慰西溟

何事添凄咽？
但由他、天公簸弄，莫教磨涅。
失意每多如意少，终古几人称屈。
须知道、福因才折。
独卧藜床看北斗，背高城、玉笛吹成血。
听谯鼓，二更彻。

丈夫未肯因人热。
且乘闲、五湖料理，扁舟一叶。
泪似秋霖挥不尽，洒向野田黄蝶。
须不羡、承明班列。
马迹车尘忙未了，任西风吹冷长安月。
又萧寺，花如雪。

YUAN MEI
(1716-1797)

On Lady Yang*

Sing not of Lady Yang's regret of days gone by!
The Silver River severs on earth as on high.
In Stone Moat Village when the man parted from his wife,
More tears were shed than in the Palace of Long Life.

* Lady Yang (719-756) was the favorite mistress of Emperor Xuan Zong of the Tang Dynasty. She lamented that they were separated from each other in the Palace of Long Life just as the two celestial lovers were separated by the Silver River (the Milky Way). But they ignored the fact that their sufferings were nothing compared with those they inflicted on their subjects (see Du Fu's "Pressgang at Stone Moat Village").

袁枚

（1716–1797）

马嵬驿

莫唱当年长恨歌，
人间亦自有银河。
石壕村里夫妻别，
泪比长生殿上多。

CAO XUEQIN (1715-1763)

Lin Daiyu's Elegy on Flowers

As flowers fall and fly across the skies,
Who rues the red that fades, the scent that dies?
Softly the gossamer floats over bowers green;
Gently the willow fluff wafts to broidered screen.

In my chamber I'm grieved to see spring depart.
Where can I pour out my sorrow-laden heart?
I step out of my portal with a hoe.
On fallen petals could I come and go?

Willow threads and elm leaves are fresh and gay;
They care not if peach and plum blossoms drift away.
The peach and plum will bloom next year.
But in my chamber who will then appear?

By the third moon the swallows built their nest,
But apathetically on the beam they rest.
Next year though they may peck the buds again,
O in my empty chamber can their nest remain?

For three hundred and sixty days each year,
The cutting wind and biting frost make flowers sear.
How long can they blossom fresh and fair?
Once blown away, they cannot be found anywhere.

曹雪芹

（1715–1763）

黛玉葬花词

花谢花飞花满天，红消香断有谁怜？
游丝软系飘春榭，落絮轻沾扑绣帘。

闺中女儿惜春暮，愁绪满怀无释处。
手把花锄出绣帘，忍踏落花来复去。

柳丝榆荚自芳菲，不管桃飘与李飞；
桃李明年能再发，明年闺中知有谁？

三月香巢已垒成，梁间燕子太无情！
明年花发虽可啄，却不道人去梁空巢也倾。

一年三百六十日，风刀霜剑严相逼；
明媚鲜妍能几时，一朝漂泊难寻觅。

Their gravedigger, I find no flowers in bloom;
My aching heart is further filled with gloom.
With hoe in hand, tears secretly shed
Like drops of blood turn bare branches red.

At twilight falls, the cuckoos sing no more;
I come back with my hoe and close the door.
Abed in dim-lit room when night is still,
I hear cold rain and my quilt feels damp and chill.

I wonder why I'm thrown in such a fret:
Is it for love of spring or for regret?
I love it when it comes, regret it when it goes;
But spring comes and goes mute as water flows.

Last night from the courtyard a dirge was heard,
Sung by the soul of flower and of bird.
The bird's and flower's soul is hard to detain;
The flowers blush and silent birds remain.

I long on wings to fly
With flowers to the end of the earth and the sky.
At earth's uttermost bound,
Where can I find a fragrant burial mound?

Why don't I shroud in silken bag the petals fair
And bury them in the earth forever to mingle there?
Pure they come and pure shall go,
Not sinking to oblivion below.

花开易见落难寻，阶前愁杀葬花人，
独倚花锄泪暗洒，洒上空枝见血痕。

杜鹃无语正黄昏，荷锄归去掩重门；
青灯照壁人初睡，冷雨敲窗被未温。

怪奴底事倍伤神？半为怜春半恼春。
怜春忽至恼忽去，至又无言去未闻。

昨宵庭外悲歌发，知是花魂与鸟魂？
花魂鸟魂总难留，鸟自无言花自羞；

愿侬此日生双翼，随花飞到天尽头。
天尽头，何处有香丘？

未若锦囊收艳骨，一抔净土掩风流。
质本洁来还洁去，强于污淖陷渠沟。

Now they are dead, I come to bury them today.
Who can divine the date when I shall pass away?
Men laugh at my folly burying many a fallen flower.
But who would bury me when came my last hour?

See spring depart and flowers wither by and by.
This is the time when beauty must grow old and die.
Once spring is gone and beauty dead, alas!
Who will care for the fallen bloom and buried lass?

尔今死去侬收葬，未卜侬身何日丧？
侬今葬花人笑痴，他年葬侬知是谁？

试看春残花渐落，便是红颜老死时；
一朝春尽红颜老，花落人亡两不知！

图书在版编目（CIP）数据

不朽的美：似曾相识燕归来：许渊冲经典英译诗词：五代－清朝．第三辑：汉英对照 / 许渊冲译．-- 北京：新世界出版社，2019.6（2021.6 重印）
ISBN 978-7-5104-6281-8

Ⅰ．①不… Ⅱ．①许… Ⅲ．①古典诗歌－诗集－中国－汉、英 Ⅳ．① I222

中国版本图书馆 CIP 数据核字 (2017) 第 100904 号

Songs of the Immortals

AN ANTHOLOGY OF CLASSICAL CHINESE POETRY (III)

不朽的美：似曾相识燕归来

许渊冲经典英译诗词（五代—清朝）

第三辑：汉英对照

译　　者：许渊冲
审　　定：王池英
责任编辑：李晨曦
特邀编辑：杨晓敏
装帧设计：贺玉婷
责任校对：宣　慧　陆诗婷
责任印制：王宝根　苏爱玲
出　　版：新世界出版社
网　　址：http://www.nwp.com.cn
社　　址：北京西城区百万庄大街 24 号（100037）
发 行 部：(010)6899 5968（电话）　(010)6899 0635（电话）
总 编 室：(010)6899 5424（电话）　(010)6832 6679（传真）
版 权 部：+8610 6899 6306（电话）nwpcd@sina.com（电邮）
印　　刷：北京亚通印刷有限责任公司
经　　销：新华书店
开　　本：880mm × 1230mm　1/32　尺寸：145mm × 210mm
字　　数：100 千字　　　　　　　　印张：8.5
版　　次：2019 年 6 月第 1 版　2021 年 6 月第 2 次印刷
书　　号：ISBN 978-7-5104-6281-8
定　　价：40.80 元
